Sophie May

Little Folks Astray

Sophie May

Little Folks Astray

ISBN/EAN: 9783744771863

Printed in Europe, USA, Canada, Australia, Japan

Cover: Foto ©ninafisch / pixelio.de

More available books at **www.hansebooks.com**

THE LOST FLY — Page 104

LITTLE PRUDY'S

FLY AWAY SERIES

LITTLE FOLKS ASTRAY

ILLUSTRATED

LEE & SHEPARD BOSTON.

LITTLE PRUDY'S FLYAWAY SERIES.

LITTLE FOLKS
ASTRAY.

BY

SOPHIE MAY,

AUTHOR OF "LITTLE PRUDY STORIES," "DOTTY DIMPLE
STORIES," ETC.

ILLUSTRATED.

" To give room for wandering is it,
That the world was made so wide."

BOSTON 1891
LEE AND SHEPARD PUBLISHERS
15 MILK STREET NEXT "THE OLD SOUTH MEETING HOUSE"

TO

MY YOUNG FRIEND,

EMMA ADAMS.

"JOHNNIE OPTIC."

TO PARENTS.

HERE come the Parlins and Cliffords again. They had been sent to bed and nicely tucked in, but would not stay asleep. They "wanted to see the company down stairs;" so they have dressed themselves, and come back to the parlor. I trust you will pardon them, dear friends. Is it not a common thing, in this degenerate age, for grown people to frown and shake their heads, while little people do exactly as they please?

Well, one thing is certain: if these children insist upon sitting up, they shall listen to lectures on self-will and disrespect to superiors, which will make their ears tingle.

Moreover, they shall hear of other people, and not always of themselves. Fly Clifford, who expects to be in the middle, will be somewhat overwhelmed, like a fly in a cup of milk; for Grandma Read is to talk her down with her Quaker speech, and Aunt Madge with her story of the summer when she was a child. It is but fair that the elders should have a voice. That they may speak words which shall come home to many little hearts, and move them for good, is the earnest wish of

THE AUTHOR.

CONTENTS.

(7)

LITTLE FOLKS ASTRAY.

CHAPTER I.

THE LETTER.

KATIE CLIFFORD sat on the floor, in the sun, feeding her white mice. She had a tea-spoon and a cup of bread and milk in her hands. If she had been their own mother she could not have smiled down on the little creatures more sweetly.

"'Cause I spect they's hungry, and that's why I'm goin' to give 'em sumpin' to eat. Shut your moufs and open your eyes," said she, waving the tea-spoon, and spattering the bread and milk over their backs.

(8)

"Quee, quee," squeaked the little mice, very well pleased when a drop happened to go into their mouths.

"What are you doing there, Miss Top-knot," said Horace: "O, I see; catching rats."

Flyaway frowned fearfully, and the tuft of hair atop of her head danced like a war-plume.

"I shouldn't think folks would call 'em names, Hollis, when they never did a thing to you. Nothing but clean white mouses!"

"Let's see; now I look at 'em, Topknot, they *are* white. And what's all this paper?"

"Bed-kilts."

"*In*-deed?"

"You knew it by-fore!"

"One, two, three; I thought the doctor gave you five. Where are they gone?"

"Well, there hasn't but two died; the rest'll live," said Fly, swinging one of them around by its tail, as if it had been a tame cherry.

Just then Grace came and stood in the parlor doorway.

"O, fie!" said she; "what work! Ma doesn't allow that cage in the parlor. You just carry it out, Fly Clifford."

Miss Thistledown Flyaway looked up at her sister shyly, out of the corners of her eyes. Grace was now a beautiful young lady of sixteen, and almost as tall as her mother. Flyaway adored her, but there was a growing doubt in her mind whether sister Grace had a right to use the tone of command.

"'Cause I 'spect she isn't my mamma."

"Why, Fly, you haven't started yet!"

"I didn't think 'twas best," responded

the child, sulkily, fixing her eyes on the mice, who were dancing whirligigs round the wheel.

"Come here to your best friend, little Topknot," said Horace. "Let's take that cage into the green-house, and ask papa to keep it there, because the mice look like water-lilies on long stems."

Flyaway brightened at once. She knew water-lilies were lovely. Giving Grace a triumphant glance, she danced across the room, and put the cage in Horace's hands, with a smile of trusting love that thrilled his heart.

"Hollis laughs at my mouses, but he don't say, 'Put 'em away,' and, '*Put* 'em away:' he says, 'Little gee-urls wants to see things as much as anybody else,'" thought she, gratefully.

"Horace," said Grace, with a curling

lip, "that child is growing up just like you — fond of worms, and bugs, and all such disgusting things."

Horace smiled. No matter for the scorn in Grace's tone; it pleased him to be compared in any way with his precious little Flyaway.

"Topknot has a spark of sense," said he, leading her along to the green-house. "I'll bring her up not to scream at a spider."

"Now, young lady," said he, setting the cage on the shelf beside a camellia, and speaking in a low voice, though they were quite alone, "*can* you keep a secret?"

"Course I can; What *is* a *secrid?*"

"Why, it's something you musn't ever tell, Topknot, not to anybody that lives."

"Then I won't, *cerdily*, — not to mamma, nor papa, nor Gracie."

"Nor anybody else?"

"No; course not. *Whobody* else could I? O, 'cept Phibby. There, now, what's the name of it."

"The name of it is—a secret, and the secret is this— Sure you won't tell any single body, Topknot?"

"No; I said, *whobody* could I tell? O, 'cept Tinka! There now!"

"Well, the secret is this," said Horace, laying his forefingers together, and speaking very slowly, in order to prolong the immense delight he felt in watching the little one's eager face. "You know you've got an aunt Madge?"

"Yes; so've you, too."

"And she lives in the city of New York."

"Does she? When'd she go?"

"Why, she has always lived there; ever since she was married."

"O, yes; and uncle Gustus was married, too; they was both married. Is that all?"

"And she thinks you and I are 'cute chicks, and wants us to go and see her."

"Well, course she does; I knew that before," said Fly, turning away with indifference; "I did go with mamma."

"O, but she means now, Topknot; this very Christmas. She said it in a letter."

"Does she truly?" said Fly, beginning to look pleased. "But it can't be a *secrid*, though," added she, next moment, sadly, "'cause we can't go, Hollis."

"But I really think we shall go, Topknot; that is, if you don't spoil the whole by telling."

"O, I cordily won't tell!" said Fly, fluttering all over with a sense of importance, like a kitten with its first mouse.

The breakfast bell rang; and, with many
a word of warning, Horace led his little
sister into the dining-room.

"Papa," said she, the moment she was
established in her high chair, "I know
sumpin'."

"O, Topknot!" cried Horace.

"I know Hollis has got his elbows on
the table. There, now, *did* I tell?"

"Hu—sh, Topknot!"

There was a quiet moment while Mr.
Clifford said grace.

"Hollis," whispered Katie immediately
afterwards, "will I take my mouses?"

"'Sh, Topknot!"

"What's going on there between you and
Horace?" laughed Grace.

"A *scerid*," said Fly, nipping her little
lips together. "You won't get me to tell."

"Horace," exclaimed Mrs. Clifford, "you
haven't—"

" Why, mother, I thought it was all settled, and wouldn't do any harm; and it
pleases her so!"

"Well, my son, you've made a hard
day's work for me," said Mrs. Clifford,
smiling behind her coffee-cup, as eager
little Katie swayed back and forth in her
high chair.

" You won't get me to tell, Gracie Clifford. She don't want nobody but Hollis
and me; she thinks we're very 'cute."

"Who? O, Aunt Louise, probably."

"No, aunt Louise never! It's the auntie
that lives to New York."

" Sh, Topknot!"

"Well, I didn't tell, Hollis Clifford!"

"So you didn't," said Grace. "But
wouldn't it be nice if somebody should ask
you to go somewhere to spend Christmas?

"Well, *there is!*"

2

"O, Topknot," cried Horace, in mock distress, "you said you could keep a secret."

Flyaway looked frightened.

"What'd I do?" cried she; "I didn't tell nuffin 'bout the letter!"

This last speech set everybody to laughing; and the little tell-tale looked around from one to another with a face full of innocent wonder. They couldn't be laughing at *her!*

"I can keep secrids," said she, with dignity. "It was what I was a-doin'."

"It is your brother Horace who cannot be trusted to keep secrets," said Mrs. Clifford, taking a letter from her pocket. "Hear, now, what your Aunt Madge has written: 'Will you lend me your children for the holidays, Maria? I want all three; at any rate, two.'"

"That's me," cried Flyaway, tipping over her white coffee; "'tenny rate two,' means me."

"Don't interrupt me, dear. 'Brother Edward has promised me Prudy and Dotty Dimple. They may have a Santa Claus, or whatever they like. I shall devote myself to making them happy, and I am sure there are plenty of things in New York to amuse them. Horace must come without fail: for the little girl-cousins always depend so much upon him.'"

A smile rose to Horace's mouth; but he rubbed it off with his napkin. It was his boast that he was above being flattered.

"But why not have Grace go, too, to keep them steady?" said Mr. Clifford, bluntly.

Horace applied himself to his buckwheat cakes in silence, and looked rather gloomy.

"Why, I suppose, Henry, it would hardly be safe to send Grace, on account of her cough."

"I'm so sorry you asked Dr. De Bruler a word about it, mamma; but I suppose I must submit," said Grace, with a face as cloudy as Horace's.

"Horace, my son, do you really feel equal to the task of taking this tuft of feathers to New York?"

"I don't know why not, father; I'm willing to try."

"Horace has good courage," said Grace, shaking her auburn curls like so many exclamation points. "I never could! I never would! I'd as soon have the care of a flying squirrel!"

"Hollis never called me a *squirl*," said Fly, demurely. "I've got two brothers, and one of 'em is an angel, and the other isn't: but Hollis is *'most* as good as the one up in the sky."

"Well, my son," remarked Mr. Clifford, after a pause, "if your mother gives her consent, I suppose I shall give mine: but it does not look clear to me yet. One thing is certain, Horace: if you do undertake this journey, you must live on the watch: you must sleep with both eyes open. Don't trust the child out of your sight—not for a moment. Don't even let go her hand on the street."

"I do believe Horace will be as careful as either you or I. Henry, or I certainly wouldn't trust him with our last little darling," said Mrs. Clifford.

His mother's words dropped like balm upon Horace's wounded spirit. He looked up, and felt himself a man again.

CHAPTER II.

THE UNDERTAKING.

WHEN Flyaway knew she was going to New York, it was about as easy to fit her dresses as to clothe a buzzing blue-bottle fly. With spinning head and dancing feet, she was set down, at last, in the cars.

"Here we are, all by ourselves, darling, starting off for Gotham. Wave your handkerchief to mamma. Don't you see her kissing her hand? There, you needn't spring out of the window! And I declare, Brown-brimmer, if you haven't thrown away your handkerchief! Here, cry into mine!"

"I didn't want to cry, Hollis; I wanted

to laugh," said the child, wiping her eyes with her doll's cloak. "When you ride in carriages, you don't get anywhere; but when you ride in the cars, you get there right off."

"Yes: that's so, my dear. You are in the right of it, as you always are. Now I am going to turn the seat over, and sit where I can look at you—just so."

"O, that's just as splendid, Hollis! Now there's only me and Flipperty. There, I put her 'pellent cloak on wrong; but see, now, I've un-*wrong-side-outed* it! Don't she sit up like a lady?"

Her name was Flipperty Flop. She was a large jointed doll (not a doll with large joints,) had seen a great deal of the world, and didn't think much of it. She came of a high family, and had such blue blood in her veins, that the ground wasn't good

enough for her to walk on. She wore a
" 'pellent cloak " and rubber boots, and had
a shopping-bag on her arm full of " choclid "
cakes. She was nearly as large as her
mother, and all of two years older. A
great deal had happened to her before her
mother was born, and a great deal more
since. Sometimes it was dropsy, and she
had to be tapped, when pints of sawdust
would run out. Sometimes it was con-
sumption, and she wasted to such a skel-
eton that she had to be revived with cot-
ton. She had lost her head more than
once, but it never affected her brains:
she was all the better with a young head
now and then on her old shoulders. Her
present ailment appeared to be small-pox:
she was badly pitted with pins and a pen-
knife.

"I declare I forgot to get a ticket for

her." said Horace. "What if the conductor shouldn't let her pass?"

"O, Hollis, but he must?" cried Fly, springing to her feet: "*I* shan't pass athout my Flipperty! Tell the 'ductor 'bout my white mouses died, and I can't go athout sumpin to carry."

"Pshaw! Dotty Dimple don't carry dolls. She don't like 'em: sensible girls never do."

"Well, *I* like 'em," said Flyaway, nothing daunted. "You knew it byfore: 'n if you didn't want Flipperty, you'd ought to not come!"

Horace laughed, as he always did when his little sister tried her power over him. The conductor was an old acquaintance, and he told him how it stood with Flipperty, how she was needed at New York, and all that; whereupon Mr. Van Dusen gave Fly a little green card, and told her to keep it to show to all the conductors on the road; for it was a free pass, and would take Flipperty all over the United States.

"Yes, sir, if you please," said Fly, with a blush and a smile, and put the "free pass" in Miss Flop's cloak pocket.

After this, she never once failed to show it, whenever Mr. Van Dusen, or any other conductor, came near, but always had to hunt for it, and once brought up a cookie instead, which fearful mistake mortified her to the depths of her soul.

Horace was sure all eyes were fixed on his charming little charge, and was proud of the honor of showing her off; but he paid for it dearly; it cost him more than his Latin, with all the irregular verbs. There was no such thing as her being

comfortable. She was full of care about
him, herself, and the baggage. Flipperty
lost off a rubber boot, which bounced over
into the next seat. Horace had to ask a
gentleman and his sick daughter to move,
and, after all, it was in an old lady's lap.

Then Fly's feet were cold, and Horace
took her to the stove; but that made her
eyes too hot, and she danced back, to lie
with her head on his breast and her feet
against the window, till she suddenly
whirled straight about, and planted her
tiny boots under his chin.

"O, Topknot, Topknot, I pity that
woman with the baby, if she feels as lame
all over as I do!"

"Where's the baby, Hollis? O, I see."

"What's the matter, now? Why upon
earth can't you sit still, child?" said Horace, next minute, catching her as she was

darting into the aisle, dragging Miss Flop by the hair of the head.

"O, Hollis, don't you see there's a dolly over there, with two girls and a lady with red clo'es on? 'Haps they'd be willing for her to get 'quainted with Flipperty?"

"Well, Topknot, 'haps they would, but 'haps I wouldn't. I can't have you dancing all over the car, in this style."

Flyaways's lip quivered, and a tear started. Horace was moved. One of Fly's tears weighed a pound with him, even when it only wet her eyelashes, and wasn't heavy enough to drop.

"Well, there, darling, you just sit still, —not still enough, though, to give you a pain (Fly always said it gave her a pain to sit still),—and I'll bring the girls and dollie over here to you. Will that do?"

Fly thought it would.

A dreadful fit of bashfulness came over Horace, when he stood face to face with the black-eyed lady and her daughters, and tried to speak.

"I've got a little girl travelling with me, ma'am; she's so—so uneasy, that I don't know what to do with her. Will you let me take—I mean, are you willing —"

"Bring her over here, and we will try to amuse her," said the black-eyed lady, pleasantly; but Horace was sure he saw the oldest girl laughing at him.

"It's no fun to go and make a fool of yourself," thought he, leading Fly to the new acquaintances, and standing by as she settled herself shyly in the seat.

"How do you do, little one? What is your name?—*Flyaway?*—Well, you look like it. We saw you were a darling, clear across the aisle. And you have a kind brother, I know."

At these words Fly, for want of some answer to make, sprang forward and kissed Horace on the bridge of the nose.

"There, you've knocked off my cap."

In stooping to pick it up, he awkwardly hit his head against the older girl, who already looked so mischievous that he was rather afraid of her.

"Wish I could get out of the way. She expects me to speak, but I shan't.

> "'Needles and pins, needles and pins,
> When a man travels his trouble begins.'"

Horace was obliged to stand, very ill at ease, till the black-eyed lady had found out where he lived, who his father was, and what was his mother's name before she was married.

"Tell your father, when you go home, you have seen Mrs. Bonnycastle, formerly

Ann Jones, and give him my regards. I knew he married a lady from Maine."

"I know sumpin," struck in Fly; "if ever *I* marry anybody, I'll marry my own brother Hollis. I mean if I don't be a ole maid!"

"And what is 'a ole maid,' you little witch?"

"I don' know; some folks is," was the wise reply. Flyaway was about to add "Gampa Clifford," but did not feel well enough acquainted to talk of family matters.

When the Bonnycastles left, at Cleveland. Horace thought that was the last of them. Miss Gerty was "decent-looking, looked some like Cassy Hallock; but he couldn't bear to see folks giggle; hoped he never should set eyes on those people again." Whether he ever did, you shall bear one of these days.

"O, Topknot," said he, "your hair looks like a mop. Do you want all creation laughing at you? You'll mortify me to death."

"You ought to water it. If you don't take better care o' your little sister, I won't never ride with you no more, Hollis Clifford!"

"Well, see that you don't, you little scarecrow," said the suffering boy, out of all patience. "If you are going to act in New York as you have on the road, I wish I was well out of this scrape."

Flyaway was really a sight to behold. How she managed to tear her dress off the waist, and loose five boot buttons, and last, but not least, the very hat she wore on her head, *would* have been a mystery if you hadn't seen her run.

When they reached the city, Horace put

the soft, flying locks in as good order as he could, and tied them up in his handkerchief.

"I wisht I hadn't come,' whined Fly; "I don't want to wear a hangerfiss; 'tisn't speckerble!"

"Hush right up! I'm not going to have you get cold!—My sorrows! Shan't I be thankful when I get where there's a woman to take care of her?"

On the platform at the depot, aunt Madge, Prudy, and Dotty Dimple, were waiting for them. A hearty laugh went the rounds, which Fly thought was decidedly silly. Aunt Madge took the young travellers right into her arms, and hugged them in her own cordial style, as if her heart had been hungry for them for many a day.

"We're so glad!—for it did seem as

if you'd never come," exclaimed Dotty
Dimple.

"And I'd like to know," said Horace
"how you happened to get here first."

"O, we came by express — came yes
terday."

"By 'spress?" cried Flyaway, pulling
away from aunt Madge, who was trying to
pin her frock together; "*we* came by a
'ductor.— Why, where's Flipperty's ticket?"

Horace seized Prudy with one hand,
and Dotty Dimple with the other, turning
them round and round.

"I don't see anything of the express
mark, 'Handle with care.' What has become of it?"

"O, we were done up in brown paper,"
said Prudy, laughing, "and the express
mark was on that; but aunt Madge took
it off as soon as she got the packages
home."

"Why, what a story, Prudy Parlin! We didn't have a speck of brown paper round us. Just cloaks and hats with feathers in!"

Dotty spoke with some irritation. She had all along been rather sensitive about being sent by express, and could not bear any allusion to the subject.

"There, that's Miss Dimple herself. Let me shake hands with your Dimpleship! Didn't come to New York to take a joke, — did you?"

"No, her Dimpleship came to New York to get warm," said Peacemaker Prudy; "and so did I, too. You don't know how cold it is in Maine."

By this time they were rattling over the stones in their aunt's elegant carriage. It was dusk; the lamps were lighted, the streets crowded with people, the shops blazing with gay colors.

"I didn't come here to get warm, either," said Dotty, determined to have the last word: "I was warm enough in Portland. I s'pose we've got a furnace, — haven't we? —and a coal grate, too."

"I do hope Horace hasn't got her started in a contrary fit," thought Prudy; "I brought her all the way from home without her saying a cross word."

But aunt Madge had a witch's broom, to sweep cobwebs out of the sky. Putting her arm around Dotty, she said, —

"You all came to bring sunshine into my house; bless your happy hearts."

That cleared Dotty's sky, and she put up her lips for a kiss; while Flyaway, with her "hangerfiss" on, danced about the carriage like a fly in a bottle, kissing everybody, and Horace twice over.

"'Cause I spect we've got there. But,

Hollis," said she, with the comical shade
of care which so often flitted across her
little face, "you never put the trunk in
here. Now that 'ductor has gone and carried off my nightie."

CHAPTER III.

THE FROLIC.

IF Aunt Madge had dressed in linsey
woolsey, with a checked apron on, she
would still have been lovely. A white
rose is lovely even in a cracked tea-cup.
But Colonel Augustus Allen was a rich
man, and his wife could afford to dress
elegantly. Horace followed her to-night
with admiring eyes.

"They say she isn't as handsome as Aunt
Louise, but I know better; you needn't
tell me! Her eyes have got the real good
twinkle, and that's enough said."

Horace was like most boys; he mistook
loveliness for beauty. Mrs. Allen's small

figure, gentle gray eyes, and fair curls
made her seem almost insignificant beside
the splendid Louise; but Horace knew better; you needn't tell *him!*

"Horace," said Aunt Madge, "your Uncle
Augustus is gone, and that is one reason,
you know, why I begged for company
during the holidays. You will be the only
gentleman in the house, and we ladies here-
with put ourselves under your protection.
Will you accept the charge?"

"He needn't *pertect* ME," spoke up Miss
Dimple, from the depths of an easy-chair;
"I can pertect myself."

"Don't mind going to the Museum alone,
I suppose, and crossing ferries, and riding
in the Park, and being out after dark?"

"No; I'm not afraid of things," replied
the strong-minded young lady; "ask Prudy if I am. And my father lets me go

in the horse-cars all over Portland. That's since I travelled out west."

Here the bell sounded, and the only gentleman of the house gave his arm to Mrs. Allen, to lead her out to what he supposed was supper, though he soon found it went by the name of dinner. Neither he nor his young cousins were accustomed to seeing so much silver and so many servants; but they tried to appear as un-concerned as if it were an every-day affair. Dotty afterwards said to Prudy and Hor-ace, "I was 'stonished when that man came to the back of my chair with the butter; but I said, '*If* you please, sir,' just as if I 'spected it. *He* don't know but my father's rich."

After dinner Fly's eyes drew together, and Prudy said,—

"O, darling, you don't know what's

going to happen. Auntie said you might sleep with Dotty and me to-night, right in the middle."

"O, dear!" drawled Flyaway; "when there's two abed, I sleep; but when there's three abed, I open out my eyes, and can't."

'So you don't like to sleep with your cousins," said Dotty, "your dear cousins, that came all the way from Portland to see you."

"Yes, I do," said Fly, quickly; "my eyes'll open out; but that's no matter, 'cause I don't want to go to sleep; I'd ravver not."

They went up stairs, into a beautiful room, which aunt Madge had arranged for them with two beds, to suit a whim of Dotty's.

"Now isn't this just splendid?" said Miss

Dimple; "the carpet so soft your boots go in like feathers; and then such pictures! Look, Fly! here are two little girls out in a snow-storm, with an umbrella over 'em. Aren't you glad it isn't you? And here are some squirrels, just as natural as if they were eating grandpa's oilnuts. And see that pretty lady with the kid, or the dog. Any way she is kissing him; and it was all she had left out of the whole family, and she wanted to kiss somebody."

"Yes," said aunt Madge.

"'Her sole companion in a dearth
Of love upon a hopeless earth.'

"If that makes you look so sober, children, I'm going to take it down. Here, on this bracket, is the head of our blessed Saviour."

"O, I'm glad," said Fly. "He'll be right there, a-looking on, when we say our prayers."

"Hear that creature talk!" whispered Dotty.

"And these things a-shinin' down over the bed: who's these?" said Flyaway, dancing about the room, with "opened-out" eyes.

"Don't you know? That's Christ blessing little children," said Dotty, gently. "I always know Him by the rainbow round His head."

"Aureole," corrected Aunt Madge.

"But wasn't it just *like* a rainbow—red, blue and green?"

"O, no; our Saviour did not really have any such crown of light, Dotty. He looked just like other men, only purer and holier. Artists have tried in vain to make his

expression heavenly enough; so they paint
him with an aureole."

Prudy said nothing; but as she looked
at the picture, a happy feeling came over
her. She remembered how Christ "called
little children like lambs to his fold," and
it seemed as if He was very near to-night,
and the room was full of peace. Aunt
Madge had done well to place such paint-
ings before her young guests; good pictures
bring good thoughts.

"All, everywhere, it's so spl-endid!" said
Fly; "what's that thing with a glass house
over it!"

"A clock."

"What a funny clock! It looks like a
little dog wagging its tail."

"That's the *penderlum*," explained Dotty; "it beats the time. Every clock has a
penderlum. Generally hangs down before

though, and this hangs behind. I declare, Prudy, it does look like a dog wagging its tail."

"Hark! it strikes eight," said Aunt Madge. "Time little girls were in bed, getting rested for a happy day to-morrow."

"I don't spect that thing knows what time it is," said Fly, gazing at the clock doubtfully, "and my eyes are all opened out: but if you want me to, auntie, I will!"

So Flyaway slipped off her clothes in a twinkling.

"We're going to lie, all three, in this big bed, Fly, just for one night," said Dotty; "and after that we must take turns which shall sleep with you. There, child, you're all undressed, and I haven't got my boots off yet. You're quicker'n a chain o' lightning, and always was."

"Why, how did that kitty get in here?"

said auntie, as a loud mewing was heard.
"I certainly shut her out before we came
up stairs."

Dotty ran round the room, with one boot
on, and Prudy in her stockings, helping
their aunt in the search. The kitten was
not under the bed, or in either of the
closets, or inside the curtains.

"Look ahind the *pendlum*," said Fly,
laughing and skipping about in high glee;
"look ahind the pendlum; look atween
the pillow-case."

Still the mewing went on.

"O, here is the kitty—I've found her,"
said auntie, suddenly seizing Fly by the
shoulders, and stopping her mocking-bird
mouth. "Poor pussy, she has turned white
—white all over!"

"You don't mean to say that was Fly
Clifford?" cried Prudy.

"Shut her up, auntie," said Dotty Dimple; "she's a kitty. I always knew her name was Kitty."

Fly ran and courtesied before the mirror in her nightie.

"O, Kitty Clifford, Kitty Clifford," she cried, "when'll you be a cat?"

"Pretty soon, if you can catch mice as well as you can mew," laughed auntie; "but look you, my dear; are you going to bed to-night? or shall I shut you down cellar?"

"Don't shut me down *cellow*, auntie," cried the mocking-bird, crowing like a chicken; "shut me in the barn with the banties."

Next moment it occurred to the child that this style of behavior was not very "speckerful;" so she hastily dropped on her knees before her auntie, and began to say her prayers. The change was so sudden, from the shrill crow of a chicken to the gentle voice of a little girl praying, that no one could keep a sober face. Prudy ran into the closet, and Dotty laughed into her handkerchief.

"There, now, that's done," said Flyaway, jumping up as suddenly as she had knelt down. "Now I must pray Flipperty."

And before any one could think what the child meant to do, she had dragged out her dolly, and knelt it on the rug, face downward, over her own lap.

"O, the wicked creature!" whispered Dotty. But Aunt Madge said nothing.

"Pray," said the little one, in a tone of command. Then, in a fine, squeaking voice, Fly repeated a prayer. It was intended to be Flipperty's voice, and Flipperty was too young to talk plain.

"There, that will do," said Aunt Madge, her large gray eyes trying not to twinkle; "did she ever say her prayers before?"

"Yes, um; she's a goody girl—when I 'member to pray her!"

"Well, dear, I wouldn't 'pray her' any more. It makes us laugh to see such a droll sight, and nobody wishes to laugh when you are talking to your Father in heaven."

"No'm," replied Flyaway, winking her eyes solemnly.

But when the "three abed" had been tucked in and kissed, Fly called her auntie back to ask, "How can Flipperty grow up a goody girl *athout* she says her prayers?"

There was such a mixture of play and earnestness in the child's eyes, that auntie had to turn away her face before she could answer seriously.

4

" Why, little girls can think and feel
you know; but with dollies it is different. Now, good night, pet; you won't
have beautiful dreams, if you talk any
more."

.

CHAPTER IV.

"TAKING OUR AIRS."

FLYAWAY awoke singing, and sprang up in bed, saying,—

" Why, I thought I's a car, and that's why I whissiled."

" But you are not a car," yawned Prudy; ' please don't sing again, or dance, either."

" It's the *happerness* in me, Prudy; and that's what dances; it's the happerness."

" That's the worst part of Fly Clifford," groaned Dotty; " she won't keep still in the morning. Might have known there wouldn't be any peace after she got here."

Dotty always came out of sleep by slow stages, and her affections were the last

part of her to wake up. Just now she did
not love Katie Clifford one bit, nor her
own mother either.

"Won't you light the lamp?" piped
Flyaway.

"Please don't, Fly," said Prudy; "don't
talk!"

"Won't you light the la-amp?"

"No, we will not," said Dotty, firmly.

"Won't you light the la-amp?"

"Is this what we came to New York
for?" moaned Dotty; "to be waked up in
the middle of the night by folks singing?"

"Won't you light the la-amp?"

"I'll pack my dresses, and go right
home! I'll — I'll have Fly Clifford sleep
out o' this room. Why, I — I —"

"Won't you light the la-amp?"

Prudy sprang out of bed, convulsed with
laughter, and lighted the gas; whereupon

Fly began to dance "Little Zephyrs," on the pillow, and Dotty to declare her eyes were put out.

"Little try-patiences, both of them," thought Prudy; "but then they've always had their own way, and what can you expect? I'm so glad I wasn't born the youngest of the family; it does make children *so* disagreeable!"

As soon as Dotty was fairly awake, her love for her friends came back again, and her good humor with it. She made Fly bleat like a lamb and spin like a top, and applauded her loudly.

"It's gl-orious to have you here, Fly Clifford. I wouldn't let you go in any other room to sleep for anything."

Which shows that the same thing looked very different to Dotty after she got her eyes open.

When the children went down to breakfast, they found bouquets of flowers by their plates.

"I am delighted to see such happy faces." said Aunt Madge. "How would you all like to go out by and by, and take the air?"

"We'd like it, auntie; and I'll tell you what would be prime," remarked Horace, from his uncle's place at the head of the table; "and that is, to take Fly to Stewart's, and have her go up in an elevator."

"Why couldn't I go up, too?" asked Dotty, with the slightest possible shade of discontent in her voice. She did not mean to be jealous, but she had noticed that Flyaway always came first with Horace, and if there was anything hard for Dotty's patience, it was playing the part of Number Two.

"We'll all go up," said Aunt Madge. "I've an idea of taking you over to Brooklyn; and in that case we shan't come home before night."

"Carry our dinner in a basket?" suggested Dotty.

"O, no; we'll go into a restaurant, somewhere, and order whatever you like."

"Will you, auntie? Well, there, I never went to such a place in my life, only once; and then Percy Eastman, he just cried 'Fire!' and I broke the saucer all to pieces."

"I've been to it a great many times," said Fly, catching part of Dotty's meaning; "my mamma bakes 'em in a freezer."

At nine o'clock the party of five started out to see New York. Aunt Madge and Horace walked first, with Flyaway between them. "We are going out to take our *airs*," said the little one.

"I don't think you need any more," said Horace, looking fondly at his pretty sister. "You're so airy now, it's as much as we can do to keep your feet on the ground."

Flyaway wore a blue silk bonnet, with white lace around the face, a blue dress and cloak, and pretty furs with a squirrel's head on the muff. She had never been dressed so well before, and she knew it. She remembered hearing "Phibby" say to "Tinka," "Don't that child look like an angel?" Fly was sure she did, for big folks like Tinka must know. But here her thoughts grew misty. All the angels she had ever heard of were brother Harry and "the Charlie boy." How could she look like them?

"Does God dress 'em in a cloak and bonnet, you s'pose?" asked she of her own thoughts.

Prudy and Dotty Dimple wore frocks of black and red plaid, white cloaks, and black hats with scarlet feathers. Horace was satisfied that a finer group of children could not be found in the city.

"Aunt Madge and I have no reason to be ashamed of them, I am sure," thought he, taking out his new watch every few minutes, not because he wished to show it, but for fear it was losing time.

"How I wish we had Grace and Susey here! and then I should have all my nieces," said Aunt Madge. "Is it possible these are the same children I used to see at Willowbrook? Here is my only nephew, that drowned Prudy on a log, grown tall enough to offer me his arm. (Why, Horace, your head is higher than mine!) Here is Prudy, who tried yesterday — didn't she? — to go up to heaven on a ladder, almost a young lady. Why, how old it makes me feel!"

"But you don't look old," said Dotty, consolingly; "you don't look married any more than Aunt Louise?"

Here they took an omnibus, and the children interested themselves in watching the different people who sat near them.

"Aren't you glad to come?" said Dotty. "See that man getting out. What is that little thing he's switching himself with?"

"That's a cane," replied Horace.

"A cane? Why, if Flyaway should lean on it, she'd break it in two. — Prudy, look at that man in the corner; *his* cane is funnier than the other one."

Horace laughed.

"That is a pipe, Dotty — a meerschaum."

"Well, I don't see much difference," said Miss Dimple; "New York is the queerest

place. Such long pipes, and such short
canes!"

Fly was too happy to talk, and sat looking out of the window until an elegantly-
dressed lady entered the stage, who attracted everybody's attention; and then
Flyaway started up, and stood on her
tiptoes. The lady's face was painted so
brightly that even a child could not help
noticing it. It was haggard and wrinkled,
all but the cheeks, and those bloomed out
like a red, red rose. Flyaway had never
seen such a sight before, and thought if
the lady only knew how she looked, she
would go right home and wash her face.

"What a chee-arming little girl!" said
the painted woman, crowding in between
Aunt Madge and Flyaway, and patting the
child's shoulder with her ungloved hand,
which was fairly ablaze with jewels; "bee-
youtiful!"

Flyaway turned quickly around to Aunt Madge, and said, in one of her very loud whispers, "What's the matter with her? She's got sumpin on her face."

"Hush," whispered Aunt Madge, pinching the child's hand.

"But there is," spoke up Flyaway, very loud in her earnestness; "O, there is sumpin on her face — sumpin red."

There was "sumpin" now on all the other faces in the omnibus, and it was a smile. The lady must have blushed away down under the paint. She looked at her jewelled fingers, tossed her head proudly, and very soon left the stage.

"Topknot, how could you be so rude?" said Horace, severely; "little girls should be seen, and not heard.

"But she speaked to me first," said Flyaway. "I wasn't goin' to say nuffin, and then she speaked."

A young gentleman and lady opposite seemed very much amused.

"I'm afraid of your bright eyes, little dear. I'll give you some candy if you won't tell me how I look," said the young lady, showering sweetmeats into Flya-way's lap.

"Why, I wasn't goin' to tell her how she looked," whispered Fly, very much surprised, and trying to nestle out of sight behind Horace's shoulder.

When they left the omnibus, the children had a discussion about the painted lady, and could not decide whether they were glad or sorry that Fly had spoken out so plainly.

"Good enough for her," said Dotty.

"But it was such a pity to hurt her feelings!" said Prudy.

"Who hurted 'em?" asked Fly, looking rather sheepish.

"Poh! her feelings can't be worth much," remarked Horace; "a woman that'll go and rig herself up in that style."

"She must be near-sighted," said Aunt Madge. "She certainly can't have the faintest idea how thick that paint is. She ought to let somebody else put it on."

"But, auntie, isn't it wicked to wear paint on your cheeks?"

"No, Dotty, only foolish. That woman was handsome once, but her beauty is gone. She thinks she can make herself young again, and then people will admire her"

"O, but they won't; they'll only laugh."

"Very true, Dotty; but I dare say she never thought of that till this little child told her."

"Fly," said Horace, " You are doing a great deal of good going round hurting folks' feelings."

" Poor woman !" said Aunt Madge, with a pitying smile ; "she might comfort herself by trying to make her soul beautiful."

" That would be altogether the best plan," said Horace, aside to Prudy ; " she can't do much with her body, that's a fact ; it's too dried up."

All this while they were passing elegant shops, and Aunt Madge let the children pause as long as they liked before the windows, to admire the beautiful things.

" Whose little grampa is that ?" cried Fly, pointing to a Santa Claus standing on the pavement and holding out his hands with a very pleasant smile ; "he's all covered with a snow-storm."

"He isn't alive," said Dotty ; " and the

snow is only painted on his coat in little dots."

" Well, I didn't spect he was alive, Dotty Dimple, only but he made believe he was. And O, see that hossy! he's dead, too, but he looks as if you could ride on him."

" This other window is the handsomest, Fly; don't I wish I had some of those beautiful dripping, red ear-rings?"

" Why, little sister," said Prudy, " I'd as soon think of wanting a gold nose as those cat-tail ear-rings. What would Grandma Read say?"

" Why, she'd say 'thee' and 'thou,' I s'pose, and ask me if I called 'em the ornaments of meek and quiet spirits," said Dotty, with a slight curl of the lip. "Auntie, is it wicked to wear jewels, if your grandma's a Quaker?"

"I think not; that is, if somebody should give you a pair; but I hope somebody never will. It is a mere matter of taste, however. O. children, now I think of it, I'll give you each a little pin-money to spend, to-day, just as you like. A dollar each to Prudy and Dotty: and, Horace, here is fifty cents for Flyaway."

"O. you darling auntie!" cried the little Parlins, in a breath. Dotty shut this, the largest bill she had ever owned, into her red porte-monnaie, feeling sure she should never want for anything again that money can buy.

"There, now, Hollis," said Fly, drawing her mouth down and her eyebrows up, "where's my skipt? *my* skipt?"

"What? A little snip like you mustn't have money," answered Horace, carelessly; "auntie gave it to me."

5

The moment he had spoken the words, he was sorry, for the child was too young and sensitive to be trifled with. She never doubted that her great cruel brother had robbed her. It was too much. Her "dove's eyes" shot fire. Flyaway could be terribly angry, and her anger was "as quick as a chain o' lightning." Before any one had time to think twice, she had turned on her little heel, and was running away. With one impulse the whole party turned and followed.

"Prudy and I haven't breath enough to run," said Aunt Madge. " Here we are at Stewart's. You'll find us in the rotunda, Horace. Come back here with Fly, as soon as you have caught her."

As soon as he had caught her!

They were on Broadway, which was lined with people, moving to and fro.

Horace and Dotty had to push their way through the crowd, while little Fly seemed to float like a creature of air.

"Stop, Fly! Stop, Fly!" cried Horace; but that only added speed to her wings.

"She's like a piece of thistle-down," laughed Horace; "when you get near her you blow her away."

"Stop, O, stop," cried Dotty; "Horace was only in fun. Don't run away from us, Fly."

But by this time the child was so far off that the words were lost in the din.

"Why, where is she? I don't see her," exclaimed Horace, as the little blue figure suddenly vanished, like a puff of smoke. "Did she cross the street?"

"I don't know, Horace. O, dear, I don't know."

It was the first time a fear had entered

either of their minds.   Knowing very little
of the danger of large cities, they had not
dreamed that the foolish little Fly might
get caught in some dreadful spider's web.

CHAPTER V.

DOTTY HAVING HER OWN WAY.

Yes, Fly was out of sight; that was certain. Whether she had turned to the right, or to the left, or had merely gone straight on, fallen down, and been trampled on, that was the question. How was one to find out? People enough to inquire of, but nobody to answer.

Horace had as many thoughts as a drowning man. How had he ever dared bring such a will-o'-the-wisp away from home? How had his mother consented to let him? His father had charged him, over and over, not to let go Fly's hand in the street. That did very well to talk about; but what could you do with a child that wasn't made of flesh and blood, but the very lightest kind of gas?

"Dotty, turn down this street, and I'll keep on up Broadway. No—no; you'd get lost. What shall we do? Go just where I do, as hard as you can run, and don't lose sight of me."

Dotty began to pant. She could not keep on at this rate of speed, and Horace saw it.

"You'll have to go back to Stewart's."

"Where's Stewart's?" gasped Dotty, still running.

"Why, that stone building on Tenth Street, with blue curtains, where we left auntie."

"I don't know anything about Tenth Street or blue curtains."

"But you'll know it when you get there. Just cross over—"

"O, Horace Clifford, I can't cross over! There's horses and carriages every minute; and my mother made me almost promise I wouldn't ever cross over."

"There are plenty of policemen, Dotty; they'll take you by the shoulder—"

"O, Horace Clifford, they shan't take me by the shoulder! S'pose I want 'em marching me off to the lockup?" screamed Dotty, who believed the lockup was the chief end and aim of policemen.

"Well, then, I don't know anything what to do with you," said Horace, in despair.

It seemed very hard that he should have the care of this willful little cousin, just when he wanted so much to be free to pursue Flyaway.

"If you won't go back to Stewart's, you won't. Will you go into this shop, then, and wait till I call for you?"

" You'll forget to call."

" I certainly won't forget."

" Well, then, I'll go in; but I won't promise to stay. I want to help hunt for Fly just as much as you do."

" Dotty Dimple, look me right in the eye. I can't stop to coax you. I'm frightened to death about Fly. Do you go into this store, and stay in it till I call for you, if it's six hours. If you stir, you're lost. Do — you — *hear?* "

" Yes, I *hear.* — H'm, he thinks my ears are thick as ears o' corn? No holes in 'em to hear with, I s'pose! Horace Clifford hasn't got the *say* o' me, though. I can go all over town for all o' him!"

" What will you have, my little lady?" said a clerk, bowing to Dotty.

" I don't want anything, if you please, sir. There was a boy, and he asked me to stay here while he went to find something."

"Very well; sit as long as you please."

"Screwed right down into the floor, this piano stool is," thought Dotty; "makes it real hard to sit on, because you can't whirl it. Guess I'll walk 'round a while. Why, if here isn't a window right in the floor! Strong enough to walk on. There's a man going over it with big boots and a cane. I can look right down into the cellar. Only just I can't see any thing, though, the glass is so thick."

Dotty watched the clerks measuring off yards of cloth, tapping on the counter, and calling out, "Cash." It was rather funny, at first, to see the little boys run; but Dotty soon tired of it.

"Horace is gone a long while," thought she, going to the door and looking out.

" He has forgotten to call, or he's forgotten where he left me, or else he hasn't found Fly. Dear, dear! I can't wait. I'll just go out a few steps, and p'rhaps I'll meet 'em."

She walked out a little way, seeing nothing but a multitude of strange faces.

"Well, I should think this was queer! I'll go right back to that store, and sit down on the piano stool. If Horace Clifford can't be more polite! Well, I should think!"

Dotty went back, and entered, as she supposed, the store she had left; but a great change had come over it. It had the same counters, and stools, and goods on lines, marked "Selling off below cost;" but the men looked very different. "I don't see how they could change round so quick," thought Dotty; "I haven't been gone *more'n* a minute."

"What shall I serve you to, mees," said one of them, with a smile that was all black eyes and white teeth. Dotty thought he looked very much like Lina *Rosenbug's* brother; and his hair was so shiny and sticky, it must have been dipped in molasses.

She answered him with some confusion. "I don't want anything. I was the girl, you know, that the boy was going somewhere to find something."

The man smiled wickedly, and said, "Yees, mees." In an instant it flashed across Dotty that she had got into the wrong store. Where was the glass window she had walked on? They couldn't have taken that out while she was gone. The floor was whole, and made of nothing but boards.

"Well, it's very queer stores should be *twins*," thought Dotty.

She entered the next one. It was not a "twin;" it was full of books and pictures.

"Why didn't Horace leave me here, in the first place, it was so much nicer. And they let people read and handle the pictures. O, they have the *goldest*-looking things!"

How shocked Prudy would have been, if she had seen her little sister reaching up to the counter, and turning over the leaves of books, side by side with grown people! Miss Dimple was never very bashful; and what did she care for the people in New York, who never saw her before? She soon became absorbed in a fairy story. Seconds, minutes, quarters; it was a whole hour before she came to herself enough to remember that Horace was to call for her, and she was not where he had left her.

"But he can't scold: for didn't he keep me waiting, too? Now I'll go back."

The next place she entered was a cigar store.

"I might have known better than to go in ; for there's that wooden Indian standing there, a-purpose to keep ladies out!"

"O, here's a 'Sample Room.' Now this *must* be the place, for it says 'Push,' on the green door, just as the other one did."

What was Dotty's astonishment, when she found she had rushed into a room which held only tables, bottles, and glasses, and men drinking something that smelt like hot brandy!

"I shan't go into any more 'Sample Rooms.' I didn't know a 'Sample' meant whiskey! But, I do declare, it's funny where *my* store is gone to."

The child was going farther and farther away from it.

"Here is one that looks a little like it.

Any way, I can see a glass window in there, on the floor."

A lady stood at a counter, folding a piece of green velvet ribbon. Dotty determined to make friends with her; so she went up to her, and said, in a low voice, " Will you please tell me, ma'am, if I'm the same little girl that was in here before? No, I don't mean so. I mean, did I go into the same store, or is this a different one? Because there's a boy going to call for me, and I thought I'd better know."

Of course the lady smiled, and said it might, or might not be the same place; but she did not remember to have seen Dotty before.

" What was the number of the store? The boy ought to have known."

" But I don't believe he did," replied Dotty, indignantly; " he never said a word

to me about numbers. I'm almost afraid
I'll get lost!"

"I should be quite afraid of it, child.
Where do you live?"

"In Portland, in the State of Maine.
Prudy and I came to New York: our
auntie sent for us—I know the place
when I see it; side of a church with ivy;
but O, dear! I'm afraid the stage don't
stop there. She's at Mr. Stewart's—she
and Prudy."

"Do you mean Stewart's store?"

"O, no'm; it's a man she knows," replied Dotty, confidently; "he lives in a
blue house."

The lady asked no more questions. If
Dotty had said "Stewart's store," and
had remembered that the curtains were
blue, and not the building, Miss Kopper
would have thought she knew what to do;

she would have sent the child straight to Stewart's.

"Poor little thing!" said she, twisting the long curl, which hung down the back of her neck like a bell-rope, and looking as if she cared more about her hair than she cared for all the children in Portland. "The best thing you can do is to go right into the druggist's, next door but one, and look in the City Directory. Do you know your aunt's husband's name?"

"O, yes'm. Colonel Augustus Allen, *Fiftieth* Avenue."

"Well, then, there'll be no difficulty. Just go in and ask to look in the Directory; they'll tell you what stage to take. Now I must attend to these ladies. Hope you'll get home safe."

"A handsome child," said one of the ladies. "Yes, from the country," replied

Miss Kopper with a sweet smile; "I have just been showing her the way home."

Ah, Miss Kopper, perhaps you thought you were telling the truth; but instead of relieving the country child's perplexity, you had confused her more than ever. What should Dotty Dimple know about a City Directory? She forgot the name of it before she got to the druggist's.

"Please, sir, there's something in here,—may I see it?—that shows folks where they live."

"A policeman?"

"No; O, no, sir."

After some time, the gentleman, being rather shrewd, surmised what she wanted, and gave her the book.

"Not that, sir," said Dotty, ready to cry.

Perhaps you will be as ready to laugh,

6

when you hear that the child really supposed a City Directory was an instrument
that drew out and shut up like a telescope,
and, by peeping through it, she could see
the distant home of Colonel Allen, on
" Fiftieth Avenue."

The apothecary did not laugh at her;
but, being a kind man, and, moreover, not
having curls hanging down his neck which
needed attention, he gave his whole care
to Dotty, found an omnibus for her, told
the driver just where to let her out, and
made her repeat her uncle's street and number till he thought there was no danger of a
mistake.

CHAPTER VI.

DOTTY REBUKED.

One would have thought that now all Dotty's troubles were over; and so they would have been, if she had not tried so hard to remember the number. She said it over and over so many times, that all of a sudden it went out of her mind. It was like rolling a ball on the ground. backward and forward, till most unexpectedly it pops into a hole. Very much frightened, Dotty bit her lip, twirled her front hair, and pinched her. left cheek—all in vain; the number wouldn't come.

"O, dear, what'll I do? I'd open that cellar door, where the driver is; but he's

all done up in a blue cape, and don't
know anything only how to whip his
horses. And there don't anybody know
where anybody lives in this city; so it's
no use to ask. For what do they care?
They'd tell you to look in the Dictionary.
There's nobody in Portland ever told me
to look in a Dictionary. Here they are,
sitting round here, just as happy, all but
me. They all live in a number, and they
know what it is; but they keep it to themselves,—they don't tell. It always makes
people feel better to know where they're
going to. When I'm in Portland I know
how to get to Park Street, and how to get
to Munjoy, and how to get to Back Cove,
with my eyes shut. But they don't make
things as they ought to in New York. You
can't find out what to do."

So the stage rumbled, and Dotty grumbled. Presently a lady in an ermine cloak got out, and Dotty did not know of anything better to do than to follow She certainly was on Fifth Avenue, and perhaps, if she walked on, she should come to the number.

" There isn't any house along here that looks like auntie's," said she, anxiously; " only they all look like it some. I never saw such a place as this city So many same things right over and over; and then, when you go into 'em, its just as different, and not the place you s'posed it was."

Here Dotty ran up some steps, and rang a bell. She thought the damask curtains looked familiar.

" No, no," cried she, running down again, as fast as the mouse ran down the clock; " my auntie don't keep onions in her bay window, I hope !"

It was hyacinth bulbs, in glass vases, which had excited Dotty's disgust.

"O, I guess I'm on the wrong side of the street; no wonder I can't find the house. There, I see a chamber window open; *our* chamber window was open. I'm going to cross over and get near enough to see if there's a little clock on the shelf that ticks like a dog wagging his tail."

No, there was no clock of any sort, and where the shelf ought to be was a baby's crib.

"Well, any way, here's that beautiful church, with ivy round it; it's ever so near auntie's; so I'll keep walking."

Dotty was right when she said the church was near auntie's — it was within three doors; but she was wrong when she kept walking precisely the wrong way. She crossed over to Sixth Avenue. Now, where

were the brown houses? She saw the
horse-cars plodding along, and tried to read
the words on them.

'Sixth Ave. and Fifty-Ninth Street.'
Why, what's an *ave?* I never heard of
such a thing before; we don't have 'aves'
in Portland. There are ever so many
people getting out of that car. While it
stops, I'll peep in, and see where it's going
to. Perhaps there's a name inside that
tells."

And, with her usual rashness, Dotty
stepped upon the platform of the car, and
looked in. What she expected to see she
hardly knew, — perhaps "Aunt Madge's
House," in gold letters; but what she
really saw was, "No Smoking;" those two
words, and nothing more.

" Well, who wants to smoke? I'm sure
I don't," thought Dotty, disdainfully, and

was turning to step off the platform, when Horace Clifford seized her by the shoulder.

"Where did you come from, you runaway?" said he, gruffly.

Close beside him were Aunt Madge and Prudy; all three were getting out of the car.

"Thank Heaven, one of them is found," cried Aunt Madge, her face very pale, her large eyes full of trouble.

Prudy kissed and scolded in the same breath. "O, Dotty Dimple, you'd better believe we're glad to see you?—but what a naughty girl! A pretty race you've led Horace, and he just wild about Fly!"

"H'm! what'd he go off for, then, and leave me there, sitting on a piano stool? S'pose I's going to sit there all day? Didn't I want to go home as much as the rest of you."

"And how did you get home? I'd like to know that," said Horace, walking on with great strides, and then coming back again to the "ladies;" for his anxiety about his little sister would not allow him to behave calmly.

"I rode."

"You weren't in the car *we* came in."

"N-o; I just happened to be peeking in there you know. But I came in an *omnibus*."

"It is wonderful," said Aunt Madge, looking puzzled, "that you ever knew what omnibus to take."

Dotty looked down to see if her boot was buttoned, and forgot to look up again.

"Well, *I* shouldn't have known one *omnibus*, as you call it, from another." said Prudy, lost in admiration. "Why, Dotty, how bright you are! And there we were, so afraid about you, and spoke to a policeman to look you up."

"I wouldn't let a p'liceman catch *me*," said Dotty, tossing her head. "But haven't you found Fly yet?"

They were at home by this time, and Horace was ringing the bell.

"No, the dear child is still missing; but the police are on her track," said Aunt Madge, looking at her watch. "It is now one o'clock. Keep a good heart, Horace, my boy. John shall go straight to the telegraph office, and wait there for a despatch. Don't you leave us, dear; we can't spare you, and you can do no good."

Horace made no reply, except to tap the heels of his boots together. He looked utterly crushed. A large city was just as strange to him as it was to Dotty, and he could only obey his aunt's orders, and

try to hope for the best. Dotty seemed
to be the only one who felt like saying a
word, and she talked incessantly.

"O, what'd you send the p'lice after her
for? To put her in the lockup, and make
her cry and think she's been naughty?
It's the awfulest city that ever I saw.
Folks might send her home, if they were
a mind to, but they won't. They don't
care what 'comes of you. There's cars and
stages going to which ways, and nothing
but 'No Smoking,' inside. And I went
and peeped in at a window, and there was
onions! And how'd I know where to go
to? There was a girl with a long curl,
and she said, 'Go to the 'pothecary's:'
and what would Fly have known where
she meant? And he looked in a Dictionary, and put me in a stage,—I was going
to tell you about that when I got ready,

—and asked me if I had ten cents, and
I had; and then I forgot what the number
was, and that was the time I saw the
onions, or I should have gone right into
somebody's else's house. And I knew there
was a church with ivy round, but Fly don't
know; she's nothing but a baby. And I
should have thought, Horace Clifford, you
might have given her that money! That
was what made her run off: you was real
cruel, and that's why I wouldn't mind
what you said. And—and—"

"Hush," said Aunt Madge, brushing back
a spray of fair curls, which the wind had
tossed over her forehead. "I don't allow
a word of scolding in my house. If you
don't feel pleasant, Dotty, you may go
into the back yard and scold into a hole."

Dotty stopped suddenly. She knew her
aunt was displeased; she felt it in the
tones of her voice.

"Dotty, the wind has been at play with your hair as well as mine. Suppose we both go up stairs a few minutes?"

"There, auntie's going to reason with me," thought Dotty, winding slowly up the staircase; "I didn't suppose she was one of that kind."

"No dear, I'm *not* one of that kind," said Mrs. Allen, roguishly; for she saw just what the child was thinking. "'I come not here to talk.' All I have to say is this: Disobey again, and I send you home immediately."

"Yes'm," said the little culprit, blushing crimson. "Now, brush your hair, and let us go down." This was the only allusion Mrs. Allen ever made to the subject; but after this, she and Dotty understood each other perfectly. Dotty had learned, once for all, that her aunt was not to be trifled with.

The child really was ashamed — thoroughly ashamed; but do you suppose she admitted it to Horace? Not she. And he, so full of anguish concerning the lost Fly, found not a word of fault; scarcely even thought of his naughty cousin at all.

CHAPTER VII.

THE LOST FLY.

Now we must go back and see what has become of the little one.

At first her heart had swollen with rage. Anger had set her going, just as a blow from a battledoor sends off a shuttlecock. And, once being started, the poor little shuttlecock couldn't stop.

"Auntie gave me that skipt. Hollis is a very wicked boy; steals skipt from little gee-urls. I don't ever want to see Hollis no more."

What she meant to do, or where to go, she had no more idea than the blue clouds overhead. She had no doubt her brother

was close behind, trying to overtake her.
Her sole thought was, that she "wouldn't
ever see Hollis no more." She knew nothing could make him so unhappy as that.
"I'll lose me, and then how'll he feel?"

"Lose me!" A wild thought, gone in
a moment; but meanwhile she was already
lost.

"I hope auntie won't give Hollis nuffin
to eat, 'cause he's took away my skipt;
nuffin to eat but meat and vertato, athout
any pie."

Flyaway shook her head so hard, that
the "war-plume" under her bonnet would
have nodded, if the air could have got at
it. "Why, where's Hollis?" said she,
looking back, and finding, to her surprise,
he was not to be seen. "I spected he'd
come. I thought I heard him walking
ahind me."

Flyaway's anger had died out by this time. It never lasted longer than a Fourth of July torpedo.

"He didn't know I runned off. Guess I'll go back, and he'll give me the skipt; and then I'll forgive him all goody."

A very nice plan; only, instead of going back, she turned a corner, and tripped along towards University Place. She had twisted her head so much in looking for Horace, that it was completely turned round. And, besides, a little farther on was a man playing a harp, and a small boy a violin. Fly paused and listened, till she no longer remembered Horace or the "skipt." She forgot this was New York, and dreamed she had come to fairy-land. Her soul was full of music. Happy thoughts about nothing in particular made her smile and clap her hands. Birds, flowers, Santa Clauses, Flipperties, and "pepnits" seemed to hover near. Something beautiful was just going to happen, she didn't know what.

After the man had played for some time without attracting attention from any body but Flyaway and a poor old beggar woman, he put his harp in a green bag, slung it over his shoulder, and walked off. Flyaway followed without knowing it. Down Sixth Avenue went the music-man, and close at his heels went she. By and by she saw a little girl, no larger than herself, with a great bundle on her shoulders.

" You don't s'pose she's got a music on *her* back?—No, not a music; it's too soft all swelled out in a bunch."

Fly went nearer the little girl, to see what she was carrying; and as she did so, some gray coals, mixed with ashes, fell out of the bundle upon her nice cloak.

"Why, she's been and carried off her mother's fireplace," thought Fly, shaking her cloak in disgust; "what you s'pose she wanted to do that for?"

But far from carrying off her mother's fireplace, the ragged little girl had only been picking up old coal out of barrels, and was taking it home to burn. It had already been burned once, and picked over and burned again, and thrown away; but perhaps this poor child's mother could coax it into a faint glow, warm enough to fry a few potatoes.

While Flyaway was shaking her cloak, and staring at some old silk dresses and bed-quilts, which were hung before a shop-door, the man with the harp on his back, and the boy with a violin under his arm,

had turned a corner, and passed out of
sight. Flyaway rubbed her eyes, and
looked again. They must have gone down
through the brick pavement, but she
couldn't see any hole. Far away in the
distance she heard their music again, and
it did not come from under ground. She
ran to overtake it, and turned into Bleecker
Street. No music-man there, but a good
supply of oranges and apples.

"Needn't folks put their hands in, and
take some out the barrels? Then why for
did the folks put 'em ou' doors?"

While pondering this grave question,
she was jostled by a man carrying a rock-
ing-chair, and very nearly fell down stairs
into an oyster-saloon. A minute more and
she was back on Broadway, the very street
where Aunt Madge and Prudy were waiting for her, but so much lower down that

she might as well have been in the State
of Maine.

"Now, I'll go find my Hollis," said she
turning another corner, and running the
wrong way with all her might. Past can-
dy-stalls, past toy-shops, past orange-
wagons. Hark, music again! Not the
soft strains of a harp, but the stirring
notes of bugle, fife, and drum. Fly kept
time with her feet.

"Here we go marchin' on," hummed
she. But the crowd "marchin' on" with
her was a strange one. Carts full of ham-
mers, pincers, and all sorts of iron tools,
and men in gray shirts, with black caps
on their heads. Some of the men had
banners, with great black words, such as
"Equal Rights," or something like them,
in German; but of course Fly could not
tell one letter from another. She only

knew it was all very "homebly," in spite
of the music. She began to think she had
better get away as soon as she could; so
she tried to cross the street, but some one
held her back; it was a lady, carrying a
small dog in her arms, like a baby.

"Don't go there, child; that's a strike,
you'll get killed."

Fly knew but one meaning for the word
strike; and, tearing herself from the lady,
ran screaming down Broadway, with the
thought that every man's hand was against
her.

On she went, and on went the strike,
close behind her. A little while ago she
had been following music, and now music
was following her. But the fifes and
drums were rather slow, and Flyaway's
feet were very swift; so it was not long
before the gray men, with their white ban-

ners and clattering carts, were far behind her. No danger now that any of the wicked creatures would strike her; so she slackened her pace.

She did begin to wonder why she had not found Horace; still, she was not at all alarmed, and there was a dreadful din in the streets, which confused her thoughts. It seemed as if people were making it on purpose. Once, at Willowbrook, she had heard boys banging tin pans, grinding coffee mills, and pounding with mortars. She had liked that,—they called it the "Calathumpian Band,"—and she liked this too; it sounded about as uproarious.

While she sauntered along, spying wonders, her eye was attracted by some balancing-toys, which a man was showing off at one of the corners. What a pleasant man he was, to set them spinning just to amuse little girls! Fly was delighted with one wee soldier, in a blue coat with brass buttons, who kept dancing and bowing with the greatest politeness. "Captain Jinks, of the horse-marines," said the toy-man, introducing him. "Buy him, miss; he'll make a nice little husband for you; only fifteen cents."

Fly felt quite flattered. It was the first time in her life any one had ever asked her to buy anything, and she thought she must have grown tall since she came from Indiana. She put her fingers in her mouth, then took them out, and put them in her pocket.

"Here's my porte-monnaie-ry," said she, dolefully; "but I haven't but two cents—no more. Hollis carried it off."

"Well, well, run along, then. Don't you see you're right in the way?"

Fly was surprised and grieved at the change in the man's tone: she had expected he would pity her for not having any money.

"Come here, you little lump of love,' called out a mellow voice; and there, close by, sat a wizened old woman, making flowers into nosegays. She had on a quilted hood as soft as her voice, but everything else about her was as hard as the door-stone she sat on.

"See my beautiful flowers," said the old crone, pointing to the table before her; "who cares for them jumping things over yonder? I don't."

The flowers were tied in bouquets — sweet violets, rosebuds, and heliotrope. Fly, whose head just reached the top of the table, smelt them, and forgot the "little husband, for fifteen cents."

"He's a cross man, dearie," said the old woman, lowering her voice, "or he wouldn't have sent you off so quick, just because you hadn't any money. Now, I love little girls, and I'll warrant we can make some kind of a trade for one of my posies."

Fly smiled, and quickly seized a bouquet with a clove pink in it.

"Not so fast, child! What you got that you can give me for it? I don't mind the money. That old pocket-book will do, though 'tain't wuth much."

It was very surprising to Fly to hear her porte-monnaie called old: for it was bought last week, and was still as red as the cheeks of the painted lady.

"I don't *dass* to give foiks my porte-monnaie-ry," said she, clutching it tighter, but holding the flowers to her nose all the while.

"O, fudge! Well, what else you got in your pocket? A handkerchief?"

"No, my hangerfiss is in my muff."

"That? Why, there isn't a speck o' lace on it. Nice little ladies always has lace. Here's a letter in the corner; what is it?"

"Hollis says it's K; stands for Fly-away."

"Well, you're such a pretty little pink, I guess I'll take it; but 'tain't wuth lookin' at," said the crafty old woman, who saw at a glance it was pure linen, and quite fine.

"Now run along, baby; your mummer will be waitin' for you."

Fly walked on slowly. Ought she to have parted with her very best hangerfiss!

"Nice ole lady, loved little gee-uris; but what you s'pose folks was goin' to cry into now?"

Tears started at the thought. One of them dropped into the eye of the squirrel, who sat on the muff, peeping up into her face.

"Nice ole lady, I s'pose; but folks never wanted to buy my *hangerfisses* by-fore!" thought Fly, much puzzled by the state of society in New York. "And I've got some beau-fler flowers to my auntie's house. Wake up—wake up!" added she, blowing open a pink rose-bud; "you's too little for me."

But the bud did not wish to wake up and be a rose; it curled itself together, and went to sleep again.

"I don't see where Hollis stays to all the time," exclaimed the little one, begin ning to have a faint curiosity about it.

CHAPTER VIII.

"THE FRECKLED DOG."

But just then a gentle-looking blind girl came along led by a dog. The sight was so strange that Flyaway stopped to admire; for whatever else she might be afraid of, she always loved and trusted a dog.

"Doggie, doggie," cried she, patting the little animal's head.

"O, *what* a sweet voice," said the blind girl, putting out her hand and groping till she touched Fly's shoulder. "I never heard such a voice!"

This was what strangers often said, and Flyaway never doubted the sweet-

ness was caused by eating so much candy;
but just now she had had none for two
days.

"What makes you shut your eyes up,
right in the street, girl? Is the *seeingness*
all gone out of 'em?"

"Yes, you darling. I haven't had any
seeingness in my eyes for a year."

"You didn't? Then you's *blind-eyed*,"
returned Flyaway, with perfect coolness.

"And don't you feel sorry for me — not
a bit?"

"No, 'cause your dog is freckled so
pretty."

"But I can't see his freckles."

"Well, he's got 'em. Little yellow ones,
spattered out all over him."

"But if I had eyes like you, I shouldn't
need any dog. I could go about the streets
alone."

"Well, I don't like to go 'bout the streets alone: I want my own brother Hollis."

"I hope you haven't got lost, little dear?"

"No," laughed Fly, gayly; "I didn't get lost! But I don't know where nobody is! And there don't nobody know where *I* am!"

The blind girl took Fly's little hand tenderly in hers.

"Come, turn down this street with me, and tell me all about it."

Fly trudged along, prattling merrily, for about a minute: then she drew away.

"'Tisn't a nice place; I don't want to go there."

A look of pain crossed the blind girl's face.

"No, I dare say you don't. It isn't much of a place for folks with silk bonnets on."

"You can't see my bonnet; you can't see anything, you're blind-eyed; but," said Fly, glancing sharply around, "it isn't pretty here, at all; and there's a dead cat right in the street."

"Yes, I think likely."

"And there's a boy. I spect he frowed the cat out the window; he hasn't nuffin on but dirty cloe's."

"Do you see some steps?" said the blind girl, putting her hand out cautiously. "Don't fall down."

"I shan't fall down; I'm going home."

"O, don't child; you must come with me. My mother will take care of you."

"I don't want nobody's mother to take 'are o' me; I've got a mamma myself!"

"How little you know!" said the blind girl, thinking aloud; "how lucky it is I found you! and O, dear, how I wish I could see! You'll slip away in spite of me."

But Flyaway allowed herself to be drawn along, step by step, partly because she liked the "freckled dog," and partly because she had not ceased being amused by the droll sight of a person walking with closed eyes.

"What's the name of you, girl?"

"Maria."

"Maria? So was my mamma; her name was Maria, when she was a little girl. O, look, there's another boy; don't you see him? Up high, in that house. Got a big box with a string to it."

A very rough-looking boy was standing at a third-story window, lowering a band-box by a clothes-line. As Fly watched the box slowly coming down, the boy called out,—

8

"Get in, little un, and I'll give you a free ride."

"O, no—O, no; I don't *dass* to."

"Yes, yes; go in, lemons," said the boy, choking with laughter, as he saw the child's horror. "If you don't do it, by cracky, I'll come down and fetch you."

At this, Fly was frightened nearly out of her senses, and ran so fast that the dog could scarcely have kept up with her, even if he had not had a blind mistress pulling him back.

"O, where are you?" exclaimed Maria. "Don't run away from me,—don't!"

"He's a-gon to kill me in two," cried Flyaway, stopping for breath: "he's a-gon to kill me in two-oo!"

"No, he isn't, dear! It's only Izzy Paul He couldn't catch you, if he tried. He's lame, and goes on crutches."

"But he said a swear word,—yes he, did," sobbed the child, never doubting that a boy who could swear was capable of murder, though he had neither hands nor feet.

"Stop, now," said Maria, clutching Fly as if she had been a spinning top. "This is my house. Mother, mother, here's a little girl; catch her—hold her—keep her!"

"Me? What should I catch a little girl for?" said Mrs. Brooks, a faded woman with a tired face, and a nose that moved up and down when she talked. She had been standing at the door of their tumble-down tenement, looking for her daughter, and was surprised to see her bringing a strange child with her. It was not often that well-dressed people wandered into that dirty alley.

"The poor little thing has got lost,

mother. Perhaps *you* can find out where she came from. I didn't ask her any questions; it was as much as I could do to keep up with her."

Maria put her hand on her side. Fast walking always tired her, for she was afraid every moment of falling.

They had to go down a flight of stairs to get into the house; and after they got there Fly looked around in dismay.

"I don't want to stay in the stable," she murmured. Indeed it was not half as nice as the place where her father kept his horse.

"But this is where we have to live," sighed Maria.

"Have things to eat?" asked the little stranger, in a solemn whisper.

There were a few chairs with broken backs, a few shelves with clean dishes, a few children with hungry faces. In one corner was a clumsy bedstead, and in a tidy bed lay a pale man.

"Who've you got there, Maria?" said he. "Bring her along, and stick her up on the bed."

"Don't be afraid," said Mrs. Brooks; "it's only pa; wouldn't the little girl like to talk to him? He's sick."

Flyaway was not at all afraid, for the man smiled pleasantly, and did not look as if he would hurt anybody. Mrs. Brooks set her on the bed, and Maria, afraid of losing her, held her by one foot. The children all crowded around to see the little lady in a silk bonnet holding a button-hole bouquet to her bosom.

"Ain't she a ducky dilver!" said the oldest boy. "Pa'll be pleased, for he don't see things much. Has to keep abed all the time."

Mr. Brooks tried to smile, and Flyaway whispered to Maria, with sudden pity,—

"Sorry he's sick. Has he got to stay sick? Can't you find the camphor bottle?"

"O, father, she thinks if you had some camphor to smell of, 'twould cure you."

Then they all laughed, and Fly timidly offered the sick man her flowers.

"What, that pretty posy for me? Bless you, baby, they'll do me a sight more good than camfire!"

"There," said Maria, joyfully, "now pa is pleased; I know by the sound of his voice. Poor pa! only think, little girl, a stick of timber fell on him, and lamed him for life!"

"Yes," said Bennie, "the lower part of him is as limber as a rag."

"She don't sense a word you say," remarked Mrs. Brooks, shaking up a pillow,

"I CAMED DOWN WHEN I WAS A BABY" - Page 129

"See what we can get out of her. What's your name, dear?"

"Katie Clifford."

"Where do you live?'

"I *have* been borned in Nindiana."

Fly spoke with some pride. She considered her birth an honor to the state.

"But where did you come from, Katie? That's what we mean."

"I camed from heaven," said the child, with one of her wise looks.

"Beats all, don't she?" cried Mr. Brooks, admiringly. "Looks like an angel, I declare for't. Did you just drop down out of the sky?"

"No, sir," answered Flyaway, folding her little hands as if she were saying her prayers; "I camed down when I was a baby."

"That's what makes your hair so *goldy*,"

said Bennie. "Mother, did you ever see such eyes? Say, did you ever? So soft, and kinder shiny, too."

"Children, don't stare at her; it makes her uneasy."

"*I* can't stare at her," said Maria, bitterly. "I suppose you don't mean me, mother."

Mrs. Brooks only answered her poor daughter by a kiss.

"Well, little Katie, after you were born in *Nindiana*, you came to New York. When did you come?"

"One of these other days I camed here with Hollis."

"Who's Hollis?"

"He's my own brother. Got a new cap. Had his hair cut."

"Who did **you** come to New York to see?"

" My auntie."

" Her auntie! A great deal of satisfaction we are likely to get out of this child," said Mr. Brooks, laughing. He had not laughed before for a week.

" What's your auntie's name ? "

" Aunt Madge."

" Is she married ? "

" O, yes; and so's Uncle 'Gustus. Married together, and live together, just the same."

" Uncle 'Gustus who ? Now we'll come at it ! "

" Alling," replied Fly, her quick eyes roving about the room, for she was tired of these questions.

" Allen, Augustus Allen ! " said Mr Brooks, in surprise; " I wonder if there can be two of them. Tell me, child, how does he look ? "

"Don't look like you," replied Fly, after a keen survey of Mr. Brooks. "Your face is pulled away down long, like that (stretching her hand out straight) "Uncle 'Gustus's face is squeezed up short" (doubling her hand into a ball)

"I'll warrant it is the colonel himself," said Mrs. Brooks, smiling at the description.

"Yes, that's the name of him; the 'kernil's' the name of him."

"Is it possible!" said Mr. Brooks, looking very much pleased.

"Uncle 'Gustus has curly hair on his cheeks, on his mouf, all round. *Not* little prickles, sticking out like needles."

"O, you girl!" said Bennie, frowning at Fly. "You mustn't laugh at my pa's beard. There's a man comes in, sometimes, and shaves him nice; but now the man's gone to Newark."

"Is it possible," repeated Mrs. Brooks, taking the child's hand, "that this is Colonel Allen's little niece, and my Maria found her!"

"Your Maria didn't find me," said Fly, decidedly; "I founded Maria."

"So she did, pa. The first thing I knew, I heard somebody calling, 'Doggie, doggie,' in such a sweet voice; and then I looked—no, of course I *couldn't* look."

Here the discouraged look came over Maria's mouth, and she said no more.

"There, there, cheer up, daughter," said Mr. Brooks, with tears in his eyes; "I was only going on to say, it is passing strange that any of our family should run afoul of one of the colonel's folks."

"It's the Lord's doings; I haven't the slightest doubt of it," said Mrs. Brooks, earnestly. "You know what I've been saying to you, pa."

"There, there, ma'am, *don't*," said Mr. Brooks; "don't go to raising false hopes You know I'm too proud to beg of any body's folks."

"Why, pa, I shouldn't call it begging just to tell Colonel Allen how you are situated! Do you suppose, if he knew the facts of the case, he'd be willing to let you suffer? Such a faithful man as you used to be to work."

"No, I think it's likely he wouldn't. He's got more heart than some rich folks; but I hain't no sort of claim on the colonel, if I did help build his house. And then, ma'am, you know I've been kind o' hopin'—"

"Guess I'll go now, and find Hollis,'

said Fly, slipping down from the bed, for the talk did not interest her.

"O, but I want to go with you, Katie," said Mrs. Brooks, coaxingly. "Bennie, you amuse her, while I change my dress."

CHAPTER IX.

MARIA'S MOTHER.

"I KNOW your uncle must feel dreadfully to lose you; but never mind—he'll see you soon," said Mr. Brooks.

" O, Uncle 'Gustus isn't there."

" Not there?" said Mrs. Brooks, turning round from the cracked looking-glass. " Where then?"

" O, he's gone off."

" Gone off? Why, pa, ain't that too bad? I'm right up and down disappointed. But, then, the colonel has a wife: I can go to see her, you know; and I'll tell her just how you're situ—"

" My Aunt Madge is gone off, too."

"You don't say so!"

"And my brother Hollis is gone."

"This is a funny piece of work if it's true." said Mr. Brooks, with another genuine laugh; "you'd better ask her a few more questions before you start out. Who else is gone? Have they shut the house up?"

"Yes, sir; shut it right up tight."

"Nobody in it, at all?"

"No, only the men and women. Prudy's gone, and Dotty Dimple's gone, and I'm gone."

"Only the men and women, she says. That must be the servants. So the house must be open, pa. At any rate, I shall take her. Say by-bye, my pretty, and we'll be starting."

Fly was very glad to go, but Maria clung to her fondly, and Bennie ran after

her almost to Broadway, where Mrs.
Brooks took a Fifth Avenue stage. She
knew Colonel Allen's house very well, for
she had seen it more than once, while it
was in process of building. That was two
or three years ago, when her husband was
well, and the family lived very comforta-
bly on Thirty-third Street. She sighed as
she thought how different it was now. Mr.
Brooks would never be able to work any
more; they hardly had food enough to eat,
and poor Maria had lost her eyesight.

"Here we are, little Katie," said she.

But the child did not wait to be helped
out; she danced down the steps, and would
have flown across the street, if Mrs. Brooks
had not caught her.

"I see it—I see it; my auntie's house.
But there isn't nobody to it."

The man who met them at the door was

so surprised and delighted to see Fly, that he forgot his manners, and did not ask Mrs. Brooks in.

"Bless us, the baby's found!" cried he, and ran to spread the news.

Aunt Madge was walking the parlor floor, and Horace sitting on the sofa, as rigid as the marble elf Puck, just over his head. Prudy and Dotty had joined hands, and were crying softly on the rug. As the police had been notified of Fly's loss, all the family had to do was to wait. A servant was at the nearest telegraph office, with a horse and carriage, and at the first tidings would drive home and report.

The words "The baby's found" rang through the house like a peal of bells. In an instant Flyaway Runaway was clasped in everybody's arms, and wet with everybody's tears.

9

"Thought I'd come back," said the little truant, peeping up at her agitated friends with some surprise; "thought I'd come back and get my skipt!"

Then they exclaimed, in chorus,—

"Topknot *shall* have her skipt! The blessed baby! The darling old Fly!"

And Dotty wound up by saying,—

"Why, you see, we thought you's dead!"

Flyaway, who had at first been very much astonished at the fuss made over her, now looked deeply offended.

"Who said I's dead? What—a—drefful —lie!"

"O, nobody said so, Fly; only we thought p'rhaps you was; and *what* would we do without you, you know?"

"Why, if I's dead," said Fly, untying her bonnet strings, "then the funy-yal would come round and take me; that's all."

"We are most grateful to you," said Aunt Madge, turning to Mrs. Brooks, "for bringing home this lost child; but do tell us where you found her."

Then Mrs. Brooks related all she knew of Fly's wanderings, the little one putting in her own explanations.

"I didn' be lost," said she sharply. "I feel jus' like frettin', when you say I's lost. 'Tis the truly truth; I's walking on the streets, and a naughty woman, she's got my hangerfiss—had ashes roses on it."

"Yes, I put some otto of rose on it this morning," said Prudy. "What a shame!"

"And I gave my flowers to the sick man. He was on the bed, with a blue bed-kilt. A girl name o' Maria, tookened me home. The seeingness is all gone out of her eyes, so she can't see."

"How long has your husband been sick?" asked Mrs. Allen of the woman, while she was taking lunch in the dining-room. "Did you tell me he knew Colonel Allen?"

Mrs. Brooks dropped her knife and fork; but her lips trembled so she could not speak. Flyaway, who sat in Horace's lap, eating ginger-snaps, exclaimed, "She wants some perjerves, auntie. She don't get no perjerves, nor nuffin nice to her house."

"'Sh!" whispered Horace. The woman looked so respectable and well bred, that it seemed a great rudeness to allude to her poverty.

But Mrs. Brooks drank some water, and then answered Aunt Madge, calmly,—

"I'm not ashamed of being poor, Mrs. Allen; it's no disgrace, for there never was an honester man than my husband, nor none that worked harder, till a beam fell on him from the roof of a house, two years ago, and he lost the use of his limbs. —Yes, ma'am; he did use to know your husband. He was one of the workmen that helped build this house. I came and looked on when he was setting these very doors."

"What is his name?" asked Aunt Madge, looking very much interested, and taking out her note-book and pencil. "What street and number?"

"Cyrus Brooks, Number Blank, Blank Street, ma'am. Before the accident, we lived on Thirty-third Street, in very good shape; but, little by little, we were obliged to sell off, and finally had to move into pretty snug quarters. But we've always got enough to eat, such as it was," added the good woman, trying not to show how much she enjoyed her lunch.

"I am very glad Providence has sent you here, Mrs. Brooks," said Aunt Madge, warmly. "I know Colonel Allen will seek you out when he comes home next week; but I shall not wait for that; I shall write him this very night."

Mrs. Brooks' heart was so full that she had to cry into a coarse purple handkerchief of Bennie's, which happened to be in her pocket, and felt very much ashamed because she could not find her voice again, or any words in which to tell her gratitude. It was just as well, though. Mrs. Allen knew words were not everything. It gave her pleasure to fill a huge basket with nice things—wine and jelly for the sick man, plain food for the family, and a pretty woolen dress for Maria, which had been intended for Mrs. Fixfax, the housekeeper.

The children looked on delighted, while

the basket was filled with these articles.
then passed over to Nathaniel, who was
going home with Mrs. Brooks. It was
amusing to watch Nathaniel, with the mon-
strous burden in his hands trying to help
Mrs. Brooks down the front steps; for Aunt
Madge was not enough of a fine lady to
send the pair around by the servants'
door.

It was pleasant, too, to watch Mrs.
Brooks's happy face, half hidden in the
hood of her water proof cloak, which kept
puffing out, in the high wind, like a sail.
She was going home to tell her husband
the Lord had heard her prayers, and she
had found a friend.

"And you may depend I never talked
so easy to anybody in my life, pa;" this
was what she thought she should say. "I
didn't *have* to beg. Mrs. Allen is one of

the Lord's own; I saw it the minute I clapped my eyes on her face."

"I am going to see that woman to morrow, and ask some questions about her blind daughter," said Aunt Madge, turning away from the window.

"Ask 'bout her nose, too."

"Whose nose, Fly?"

"The woman's. It keeps a-moving when she talks."

"There, who else noticed that?" exclaimed Horace, tossing his young sister aloft. "It takes Fly, with her little eye, to see things."

"But I didn't ask her nuffin 'bout it, though, Horace Clifford. God made her so, with a wire in."

Everybody smiled at the notion of Mrs. Brooks being a wax doll.

"What a queer day it has been!" said

Prudy. "Nothing but hide and seek. We'll all keep together next time, and lock hands tight."

"Of course," said Dotty, quickly; "but look here; don't you think 'twould be safer not to let Fly go with us? She was the one that made all the fuss."

"Want to know if she was," said Horace, slyly. "Guess there are two sides to that story."

"At any rate," struck in Aunt Madge, "Fly was the one that did the most business. You went round doing good — didn't you, dear?"

"Little city missionary," said Horace.

Whereupon Miss Fly modestly dropped her head on her brother's shoulder. She concluded she had done something wonderful in running after a dog.

"On the whole," continued auntie, "we've

all had a very hard time. It's only three o'clock; but seems to me the day has been forty hours long. Let us rest, now, and have a quiet little evening, and go to bed early."

CHAPTER X.

FIVE MAKING A CALL.

THE next morning everybody felt fresh, and ready for new adventures.

"All going but the cat," said Fly, never doubting that her own company was most desirable.

"Look up in my eyes, little Topknot with the blue bonnet on. Will you run away from brother Hollis again?"

"Not if you don't take my skipt," replied Fly, looking as innocent as a spring violet.

"And look up in *my* eyes, Horace Clifford. Will you run away from Cousin Dotty, again?" said Miss Dimple, in a hurry

to speak before Aunt Madge came up to
them, and before Horace had time for a
joke.

"I didn't run away from you, young
lady, but I ran *after* you, if I remember,'
said Horace, dryly. "I don't mean to pursue you with my attentions to-day. You
seem to be able to take care of yourself."

"Look," cried Aunt Madge, coming up
to them with Prudy; "did you ever before
see a span of horses with a dog running
between them?"

"Never," said Doty; "what splendid
horses! and don't the dog have to trot, to
keep up? How do you suppose he happened to get in there?"

"O, he has been trained to it; dogs
often are. Now, my young friends, it
seems we have started for Brooklyn again;
but on our way to Fulton Ferry, I would

like to stop and see the Brooks family.
We must all go together, though. 'United
we stand, divided we fall.' "

"That's so," said Horace, as they entered
the stage. "But, auntie, do you have
perfect faith in the story that woman tells?
Perhaps her husband is only just lazy, and
her daughter shams blindness. You know
what humbugs some of 'em are. I've read
there's something they rub over their eyes,
that gives 'em the appearance of being as
blind as a bat."

Prudy looked up at Horace with admiration and respect. He spoke like a person
of deep wisdom and wide experience.

"We will see for ourselves what we
think of the fami'y," said Aunt Madge.

"Now," said she, after they had ridden
a mile or two, "we must get out here, and
walk a few blocks to the house. Fly, hold
your brother's hand tight."

"There's the chamer where the boy lives that says swear words; and there's the boy, ahind the window."

"Have a free ride, little girl?" shouted Izzy Paul, laughing; for he remembered faces as well as Fly did, and saw at once that it was the same child he had frightened so the day before. But Fly never knew fear where Horace was; she clung to him, and peeped out boldly between her fingers.

When they went "down cellow," as she called it, into Mr. Brooks's house, Aunt Madge was surprised to see how bare it looked. But Dotty Dimple need not have held her skirts so tightly about her, and brushed her elbow so carefully when it hit against the wall; for the house was as clean as hands could make it.

"Mrs. Brooks, I hope you will forgive

me for coming down upon you with this little army," said Mrs. Allen, with such a cheery smile that the sick man on the bed felt as if a flood of pure sunshine had burst into the room. He was so tired of lying there, day after day, like a great rag baby, and so glad to see anybody, especially the good lady who, his wife said, was "so easy to talk to!"

"Auntie, look! see the freckled doggie; and there's my flowers, true's you live," cried Flyaway.

"Yes, pa wanted them in a vial, close to his bed; it's the first he's seen this winter," said Maria, stroking Fly as if she had been a kitten.

"You may be sure, little lady, it will be as I said; they'll cure me full as quick as camphire. And, thank the Lord, I can see as well as smell," said Mr. Brooks,

with a tender glance at Maria which made
Horace feel ashamed of himself. The idea
of that poor child's rubbing anything into
her eyes? Why, she looked like a wounded bird that had been out in a storm. Her
face was really almost beautiful, but so sad
that you could not see it without a feeling
of pity.

"She looks as if she was walking in her
sleep," thought Prudy, and turned away
to hide a tear; for somehow there was a
chord in her heart that thrilled strangely.
That "slow winter" came back to her with
a rush, and she was sure she knew how
Maria felt.

"She is blind, and I was lame; but it
is the same kind of a feeling. O, how I
wish I could help her!"

Dotty was as sorry for Maria as she
knew how to be, but she could not be

as sorry as Prudy was; for she had
never had any trouble greater than a sore
throat.

"I don't see why the tears don't come
into my eyes as easy as they do into Prudy's," thought she, trying to squeeze out
a salt drop; "Mrs. Brooks'll think I don't
care a speck; but I do care."

As for wee Fly, she took Maria's blindness to heart about as much as she did
the murder of the Hebrew children off in
Judea.

"Pitiful 'bout her seeingness; but I
wished I had such a beauful dog!"

Aunt Madge was struck with the ex-
alted expression of Maria's face. The child
was only thirteen, but suffering had made
her look much older.

"My child," said she, putting her arm
around the little girl, and drawing her

10

towards her, "I know you see a great deal with your mind, even though your eyes are shut. Now, do tell me all about your misfortune, and how it happened, for I came on purpose to hear."

"Yes, we camed to purpose to hear," said Fly, from the foot-board of the bed, where she had perched and prattled every moment since she came in. "I founded Maria, and then I went up to her, and says I, 'Doggie, doggie!'"

"That was a pretty way to speak to her, I should think," said Dotty; "but can't you just please to hush while auntie is talking?"

"As near as I can tell the story," said Mrs. Brooks, rattling the poor old coal-stove,—for she always had to be moving something else, as well as her nose, when she talked,—"she lost her sight by studying too hard, and then getting cold in her eyes."

"She was always a master hand to study," put in Mr. Brooks.

Maria looked as if she wanted to run and hide. She did not like to have her father praise her before people.

" Yes," said Mrs. Brooks, setting a chair straight; "and by and by the *lids* began to draw together, and she couldn't keep 'em open; and there was such a pain in her eyes, too, that I had to be up nights, bathing 'em in all kinds of messes."

" *Don't* her nose jiggle?" whispered Fly to Horace.

"Of course you took her to a good physician?"

" Well, yes; we thought he was good. We went to three, off and on, but she kept growing worse and worse. It was

about the time her father was hurt, and
we spent an awful sight on her, till we
couldn't spend any more."

"And it was all a cheat and a swindle,"
exclaimed Mr. Brooks, indignantly. " We'd
better have spent the money for a horse-
whip, and whipped them doctors with it!"

"Don't, pa, don't! You see, Mrs. Allen, he gets so excited about it he don't
know what he says."

"I wonder you did not take her to the
City Hospital, Mrs. Brooks. There she
could be treated free of expense."

"The fact is, we didn't dare to," replied Mrs. Brooks, taking up an old shoe
of Bennie's, and beginning to brush it;
"there are folks that have told us it ain't
safe; they try experiments on poor folks."

"O, I don't believe you need fear the
City Hospital," said Mrs. Allen; "the phy-

sicians there are honest men, and among the
most skillful in the country."

"But that's our feeling on the subject,
ma'am, you see," spoke up Mr. Brooks,
so decidedly, that Aunt Madge saw it was
of no use to say any more about it. "We
don't want her eyes put out; there are
times when she can just see a little glim-
mer, and we want to save all there is
left."

"There are times when she can see?
Then there must be hope, Mr. Brooks!
Let me take her to Dr. Blank; he can
help her if any one can.'

"Well, now, I take it you're joking,
Mrs. Allen. That is the very doctor I
wanted her to see in the first place; but
they do say he'd ask six hundred dollars
for looking into her eyes while you'd wink
twice."

"You have been misinformed, Mr Brooks; he never asks anything of people who are unable to pay him. But even if he should in Maria's case, I promise to take the matter into my own hands, and settle the bill myself."

"Mother, do you hear what she says!" cried Mr. Brooks, forgetting himself, and trying to sit up in bed.

But his wife had broken down, and was polishing Bennie's shoe with her tears.

"O, will you take me? Can I go to that doctor?" cried Maria, forgetting her timidity, and turning her sightless eyes towards Mrs. Allen with a joyful look, which seemed to glow through the lids.

"Yes, dear child, I will take you with the greatest pleasure in life; but remember, I don't promise you can be cured. Come with your mother, to-morrow morn-

ing, at ten. Will that do, Mrs. Brooks?
And now, good by, all. Children, we must
certainly be going."

"God bless her," murmured the sick
man, as the little party passed out.

"Didn't I tell you she was an angel?"
said his wife.

"No, mother; it's that little tot that's
the 'angel.' The Lord sent her on ahead
to spy out the land; and afterwards there
comes a flesh-and-blood woman to see it
laid straight."

"Pa thinks that baby is a spirit made
out of air," said Maria, laughing in high
excitement. "And, mother, don't you
really believe now the Lord did send her,
just as much as if she dropped down out of
the sky?"

"Yes, I hain't a doubt of it, Maria,
but what the Lord had us in his mind

when he let the child slip off and get lost.— Pa, I'm going to give you some of that blackberry cordial now: you look all gone."

CHAPTER XI.

" THE HEN-HOUSES."

While the Brooks family were talking so gratefully, and Maria counting over the cookies and cups of jelly for the twentieth time, Fly, was holding on to Horace's thumb, saying, as she skipped along, —

"I hope the doctor'll take a knife, and pick Maria's eyes open, so she can see."

"Precious little *you* care whether she can see or not," said Dotty. "I don't think Fly has much feeling, — do you, Prudy? — not like you and I, I mean!"

"Pshaw! what do you expect of such a baby?" said Horace, indignantly. "You never saw a child so full of pity as this one is, when she knows what to be sorry for. But a great deal she understands about blindness! And why should she? — Look here, Topknot; which would you rather do? Have your eyes put out, and lots of candy to eat, *or*, your eyes all good, and not a speck of candy as long as you live?"

" I'd ravver have the candy *'thout* blind-eyed?"

" But supposing you couldn't have but one ?"

Fly reflected seriously for half a minute, and then answered,

" I'd ravver have the candy *with* blind-eyed !"

" There, girls, what did I tell you ?"

" 'Cause I could eat the candy athout looking, you know," added Fly, shutting her eyes, and putting a sprig of cedar in her mouth, by way of experiment.

"You little goosie," said Prudy; "when Aunt Madge was crying so about Maria, I did think you were a hard-hearted thing to look up and laugh; but now, I don't believe you knew any better."

"Hard-hearted things will soften," said auntie, kissing the baby's puzzled face. " Little bits of green apples, how hard they are! but they keep growing mellow."

"O, you little green apple," cried Dotty, pinching Fly's cheek.

"I was rather hard-hearted, if I remember, when I was an apple of that size," continued Aunt Madge. "I could tell you of a few cruel things I said and did."

" Tell them," said Horace; " please 'fess."

" Yes, auntie, naughty things are so interesting. Do begin and tell all about it."

"Not on the street, dears. Some time, during the holidays, I may turn story-teller, if you wish it; but here we are at the ferry; now look out for the mud."

"O, what a place," cried Fly, clinging to Horace. and trying to walk on his boots. "Just like where grampa keeps his pig!"

"How true, little sister! but you needn't use my feet for a sidewalk. I'll take you up in my arms. It snowed in the night; but that makes it all the muddier."

"Yes, it doesn't do snow any good to fall into New York mud," said Aunt Madge: "it is like touching pitch."

"I thought it felt like pitch," remarked Dotty: "sticks to your boots so."

"But, then, overhead how beautiful it is!" said Prudy. "I should think the dirty earth would be ashamed to look up at such a clear sky."

"But the sky don't mind," returned Horace; "it always overlooks dirt."

"How very sharp we are getting!" laughed auntie; "we have begun the day brilliantly. Any more remarks from anybody?"

"I should like to know," said Dotty, "what all those great wooden things are made for? I never saw such big hen-houses before!"

"Hear her talk!" exclaimed auntie "Hen-houses, indeed! Why, that is Fulton Market. I shall take you through it when we come back. You can buy anything in there, from a live eel to a book of poetry."

"'In mud eel is,'" quoted Horace. "Reckon I'll buy one, auntie, and carry it home in a piece of brown paper. I believe Dotty is fond of eels."

"Fond of eels! Why, Horace Clifford, you know I can't bear 'em, any more'n a snake. If you do such a thing, Horace Clifford!"

Here Prudy gave her talkative sister a pinch; for they were surrounded by people, and Aunt Madge was giving ferry-tickets to a man who stood in a stall, and brushed them towards him into a drawer.

"Does he stay in it all night?" whispered Fly; "he can't lie down, no more'n a hossy can."

"Here, child, don't try to get down out of my arms. I must carry you into the boat. Do you suppose I'd trust those wee, wee feet to go flying over East River?"

"For don't we know she has wings on her heels?" said Aunt Madge.

Fly twisted around one of her little rubbers, and looked at it. She understood the joke, but thought it too silly to laugh at. East River lay smiling in the sun, white with sails.

"Almost as pretty as our Casco Bay," said Dotty. "'Winona;' is that the boat we are going in? But, Horace, you must cross to the other side, where it says 'Gentlemen's Cabin.'"

"How kind you are to take care of me! Wish you'd take as good care of yourself, Cousin Dimple."

And Horace walked straight into the "Ladies' Cabin." There were more men in it, though, than womem; so he had the best side of the argument.

"Horace," said Aunt Madge, as they seated themselves, "where is your money?"

"Money? O, in the breast pocket of my coat."

"But don't you remember, my boy, I

advised you to leave it at home? See
that placard, right before your eyes."

"'Beware of Pickpockets!'" read Horace.
" Well, auntie, I intend to beware."

Mrs. Allen did not like his lord-of-crea-
tion tone. It was not exactly disrespect-
ful. He adored his aunt, and did not
mean to snub her. At the same time
he had paid no attention to her advice,
and his cool, self-possessed way of setting
it one side was very irritating. If Mrs.
Allen had not been the sweetest of women,
she would have enjoyed boxing his ears.

"I wish he was two years younger, and
then he would have to obey me," thought
she; "but I don't like to lay my com-
mands on a boy of fourteen."

The truth was, Horace had a large
swelling on the top of his head, known
by the name of self-esteem; and it had

got bruised a little the day before, when he was obliged to stand one side, and let his aunt manage about finding Flyaway.

"I suppose she thinks I'm a ninny, just because I don't understand this bothersome city; but I reckon I know a thing or two, if I don't live in New York!"

And the foolish boy really took some satisfaction in slapping his breast pockets, and remarking to his friends,—

"'Twould take a smart chap to get his hand in there without my knowing it. O, Prudy, where's your wallet? And yours, Dotty? I can carry them as well as not. There's no knowing what kind of a muss you may be getting into before night."

Prudy gave up hers without a word, but Dotty demurred.

"I guess I've got eyes both sides my

head, just the same as Horace has, if I am a girl."

She and Cousin Horace usually agreed, but this visit had begun wrong.

"Very well, Dot; if you think 'twould be any consolation to you to have somebody come along with a pair of scissors, and snip off your pocket, I don't know as it's any of my business."

"See if they do," replied Dotty, clutching her pocket in her right hand.

They had been speaking in loud tones, and perhaps had been overheard; for two men, on the same seat, began to talk of the unusual number of robberies that had happened within a few days and to wonder "what we were coming to next." In consequence of this, Dotty pinned up her pocket. When they reached Brooklyn, she gave her left hand to Horace, in stepping off the boat, and walked up Fulton Street, with her right hand firmly grasping the skirt of her dress.

"Good for you, Dimple!" said Horace, in a low tone; "that's one way of letting people know you've got money. Look behind you! There's been a man following you for some time."

"Where? O, where?" cried Dotty, whirling round and round in wild alarm; "I don't see a man anywhere near."

"And there isn't one to be seen," said Aunt Madge, laughing; "there's nobody following you but Horace himself. He had no right to frighten you so."

"Horace!" echoed Dotty, with infinite scorn; "I don't call *him* a man! He's nothing but a small boy!"

"A small boy!" She had finished the business now.

"The hateful young monkey!" thought Horace. "I shouldn't care much if she did have her pocket picked."

If he had meant a word of this, which he certainly did not, he was well paid for it afterwards.

They went to Greenwood Cemetery, which Dotty had to confess was handsomer than the one in Portland. Fly thought there were nice places to "hide ahind the little white houses," which frightened her brother so much, that he carried her in his arms every step of the way. After strolling for some time about Greenwood, and taking a peep at Prospect Park, they left the "city of churches," and entered a crowded car to go back to the ferry.

"Look out for *our* money," whispered Prudy; "you know auntie says a car is the very place to lose it in."

"Yes; I'll look out for your pile, Prue, though I dare say you don't feel quite so easy about it as you would if Dot had it."

"Now, Horace, don't be cross; you know it isn't often I have so much money."

Aunt Madge here gave both the children a very expressive glance, as much as to say,—

"Don't mention private affairs in such a crowd."

Colonel Allen said if his wife had been born deaf and dumb nobody would have mistrusted it, for she could talk with her eyes as well as other people with their tongues.

When they were on the New York side once more, Mrs. Allen said,—

"Now I will take you through Dotty's hen-houses. What have we here? O, Christmas greens."

A woman stood at one of the stands, tying holly and evergreens together into long strips, which she sold by the yard.

"We must adorn the house, children. I will buy some of this, if you will help carry it home."

"Load me down," said Horace; "I'll take a mile of it."

"Loaden me down, too; *I'll* take it a mile," said Fly.

"Give me that beautiful cross to carry, auntie."

"Are you willing to carry crosses, Pruly? Ah, you've learned the lesson young!"

"I like the star best," said Dotty; "why can't they make suns and moons, too!"

"Will you have a *hanker*, my pretty miss?" said the woman, dropping a courtesy.

"I never heard of a *hanker*; it looks some

like a kettle-hook. Let's buy it; see how nicely it fits on Fly's shoulder."

" It would look better for Fly to sit on the anchor," said Mrs. Allen, smiling. " It is droll enough to see such a big thing walking off with a little girl under it. Come, children, we have bought all we can carry."

" Thank you kindly, lady," said the evergreen woman, with another courtesy.

" I don't see why she need thank you kindly, auntie," said Dotty. " You wouldn't have bought her wreaths if you hadn't liked 'em."

They walked through a long space lined with such nice things that the children's mouths watered — oranges. figs. grapes. pears, French chestnuts larger than oil-nuts, and, as if that were not enough, delicious-looking pies, cakes, cold ham, and doughnuts. On little charcoal stoves stood coffee-pots; and there was a great clattering of plates and cups and saucers, which men were washing in little pans, and wiping on rather dark towels.

"It strikes me I should enjoy going into one of those cuddy-holes and eating my dinner," said Horace. "I feel about starved."

"You have a right to be hungry. It is two o'clock. How would you like some oysters? In here is a large room, with tables; rather more comfortable than these 'cuddy-holes,' as you call them."

"Only not nice," said Prudy. "O, Horace, if you should go once to an oyster saloon in Boston, you'd see the difference!"

"The probability is, I've been in Boston saloons twice to your once, ma'am."

Which was correct. She had been once, and he twice.

CHAPTER XII.

" GRANNY."

Aunt Madge seated her four guests at
a little table.

" Will you have oysters or scallops ?"

" What are scallops ?"

" They are a sort of fish; taste a little
like oysters. They come out of those
small shells, such as you've seen pin-cush-
ions made of."

The children thought they should prefer
oysters: and after the stews were ordered,
Mrs. Allen went out, and soon returned
with a dessert of cake, pie, and fruit.

" I thought I would bring it all at once,"
said she, "just what I know you will like,

and then sit down and be comfortable.
We'll lay the wreaths under the table.
There are no napkins, girls (this isn't
Boston, you know); so you'd better tuck
your handkerchiefs under your chins."

"But is this the handsomest place they've
got in New York, without any carpet to
it?" whispered Dotty.

"We'll see, one of these days," replied
auntie, with a smile that spoke volumes.

It was a very jolly dinner, and Mrs.
Allen had to send for three plates of scallops; for the children found, after tasting
hers, that they were very nice; all but
Fly, who did not relish them, and thought
it was because she did not like to eat pin-
cushions.

"Now, little folks, if you have eaten
sufficiently, and are thoroughly rested, shall
we start for home? I think a journey to

Brooklyn is about enough for one day —
don't you?   But you musn't leave without
seeing Granny."

"Granny?"

"Yes, I call her so, and it pleases her.
She has had a little table in the market
for a long while, and I like to buy some
of her goodies just to encourage her, for
she has such a way of looking on the
bright side that she wins my respect.
Listen, now, while I speak to her."

Auntie's old woman had on a hood and
shawl, and was curled up in a little heap,
half asleep.

"Pleasant day," said Mrs. Allen, going
up to the table.

"Yes, mum; nice weather *underfut*," returned the old woman, rousing herself, and
rubbing an apple with her shawl.

"And how do you do, Granny?"

"Why, is that you?" said she, the sun coming out all over her face. "And how've you been, mum, since the last time I've seen yer?"

"Very well, Granny; and how do things prosper with you?"

"O, *I'm* all right! I've had a touch of rheumaty, and this is the fust I've stirred for two weeks."

"Sorry to hear it, Granny. Rheumatism can't be very comfortable."

"Well, no; it's bahd for the jints," said the old woman, holding up her fingers, which were as shapeless as knobby potatoes.

"Poor Granny! How hard that is!"

"Well, they be hard, and kind o' stiff-like. But bless ye," laughed she, "that's nothing. I wouldn't 'a' cared, only I's afeared I'd lose this stand. There was a gyurl come and kep' it for me, what time she could spare."

"I'm glad you havn't lost the stand, Granny; but I don't see how you can laugh at the rheumatism."

"Well, mum, what'd be the use to cry? Why, bless ye, there's wus things'n that! As long's I hain't got no husband, I don't feel to complain!"

She shook her sides so heartily at this, that Fly laughed aloud.

"So you don't approve of husbands, Granny?"

"No more I don't, mum; they're troublesome craychers, so fur as I've seen."

"But don't you get down-hearted, living all alone?"

"O, no, mum; I do suppose I'm the happiest woman in the city o' New Yorruk. When I goes to bed, I just gives up all my thrubbles to the Lord, and goes to sleep."

" But when you are sick, Granny?"

"O, then, sometimes I feels bahd, not to be airnin' nothin', and gets some afeard o' the poorhouse; but, bless ye, I can't help thinking the Lord'll keep me out."

"I'm pretty sure He will," said Aunt Madge, resolving on the spot that the good old soul never should go to a place she dreaded so much. " Have you any butter-scotch to-day, Granny?"

"O, yes, mum; sights of it. Help your-self. I want to tell you something'll please you," said the old woman, bending forward, and speaking in a low tone, and with spar-kling eyes. "I've put some money in the bank, mum; enough to bury me! *Ain't* that good!"

Prudy and Dotty were terribly shocked.

She must be crazy to talk about her own funeral. As if she was glad of it, too? But Horace thought it a capital joke.

"That's a jolly way to use your money," whispered he to Prudy; "much good may it do her?" And then aloud, in a patronizing tone, "I'll take a few of your apples, Granny. How do you sell 'em?"

"These here, a penny apiece; them there, two pennies; and them, three."

Horace felt in his coat pocket for his purse; and drew out his hand quickly, as if a bee had stung it.

"Why, what! What does this mean?"

"What is it, Horace?"

"Nothing, auntie, only my wallet's gone," replied the boy, very white about the mouth.

"Gone? Look again. Are you sure?"

"Yes, as sure as I want to be?"

"Mine, — is mine gone too?" cried Prudy.

Horace did not seem willing to answer.

" Where did you have your purse last?"

" Just before we came out of Dorlon's oyster saloon. Just before we came here for butter-scotch," replied Horace, glaring fiercely at Granny.

" Are you quite sure?"

" Is mine gone, too?" cried Prudy again. " Did you put mine in the same pocket?"

"Yes, Prue; I put yours in the same pocket; and it's gone, too."

"O, Horace!"

" A pretty clean sweep, Prue."

" The *vilyins!*" cried Granny; looking, auntie thought, as if her whole soul was stirred with pity for the children · but, as Horace thought, as if she were trying to put a bold face on a very black crime.

12

"Let us go back to Dorlon's, and ask the waiters if you dropped it in there," suggested Aunt Madge.

"Yes, but *i know I didn't,*" said Horace, with another scowl at Granny.

"*My* money is safe," said self-righteous Dotty, as they walked away; "don'tyou wish you *had* given yours to me, Prudy?"

"The deceitful old witch!" muttered Horace; meaning Granny, of course.

And lo, there she stood close behind them! She was beckoning Mrs. Allen back to her fruit-stand.

"Wait here one minute, children; I'll be right back."

"Nothin', mum," said Granny, looking very much grieved; "nothin' only I wants to say, mum, if that youngster thinks as I took his money, I wisht you'd sarch me."

"Fie, Granny! Never mind what a boy like that says, when he is excited. I know you too well to think you'd steal."

"The Lord bless you, mum," cried the old woman, all smiles again.

"And, Granny, I mean to come here next week, and I'll bring you some flannel and liniment for your rheumatism. Where shall I leave them if you're sick, and can't be here?"

"O, thank ye, mum; thank ye kindly The ain't many o' the likes of you, mum. And if ye does bring the things for my rheumaty, and I ain't here, just ye leave 'em with the gyurl at this stand, if yer will."

"Did she give it back?" cried Horace, the moment his aunt appeared.

"No, my boy; how could she when she hadn't it to give?"

" But, auntie, I'm up and down sure I felt that wallet in my breast-pocket, when we came out of Dorlon's," persisted Horace. "I don't see how on earth that old woman contrived it; but I can't help remembering how she kept leaning forward when she talked ; and once she hit square against me.   And just about that time I was drawing out my handkerchief to wipe my nose."

" Yes, he did!   He wiped his nose. And the woman tookened the money; I saw her do it."

" There, I told you so!"

" You saw her, Miss Policeman Flya-away?" said Aunt Madge.   "And pray how did she take it?"

"Just so,—right in her hand."

" O, you mean the money for the butter-scotch, you little tease!"

"Yes," replied the child, with a roguish twinkle over the sensation she had made.

"Just like little bits o' flies," said Dotty. "Don't care how folks feel. And here's her brother ready to cry; heart all broken."

"Needn't be concerned about my heart, Dot; 'tisn't broken yet; only cracked. But how anybody could get at my pocket, without my knowing it, is a mystery to me, unless Granny is a witch.

"Horace, I pledge you my word Granny is innocent."

"And I'm sure nobody else could take it, auntie. The clerks at Dorlon's had no knowledge of the money; neither had any of the apple or pie merchants along the market. Things look darker for us, Prue; but I will give you the credit of behaving like a lady. And one thing is sure—

the moment I get home to Indiana I shall send you back your money."

" Horace," said Aunt Madge, " I am very suspicious that you lost your purse in one of those cars, on the Brooklyn side."

" But, auntie, I tell you there couldn't anybody get at my pockets without my knowing it ! "

"Just as Prudy told you you would, you lost it in that car," echoed Dotty. " Don't you remember what you said, Prudy ? "

" That's right; hit him again," growled Horace.

" Now, Dotty," said Prudy, suppressing a great sob in her effort to " behave like a lady," " what's the use ? Don't you suppose Horace feels bad enough without being scolded at ? "

" Auntie don't scold, nor Prudy don't,

'cause he didn't mean to lose it," said Fly, frowning at Dotty, and caressing Horace, with her hands full of evergreens.

" Besides, he has lost more than I have," continued Prudy.

" Well, a trifle more! Fifty times as much, say. I shouldn't care a fig,—speaking figuratively,—only it was all I had to get home with."

" Don't fret about that," said Aunt Madge; " I'll see that you go home with as full a purse as you brought to my house."

"O. auntie, how can I thank you? But you know father never would allow that!"

" I could tell you how to thank me," thought Mrs. Allen, though she was so kind she would *not* tell; " you could thank me by saying, 'Auntie, I've been a naughty boy.'"

But Horace had no idea of making

such a confession as that. "The money'll come up," said he; "I'm one of the lucky kind. Let's see; wouldn't it be best to advertise?"

"Thieves won't answer advertisements," said Mrs. Allen.

"But, I tell you, auntie, I dropped that wallet. I could take my oath of it."

"Well, in such a case an advertisement is the proper thing. But, my boy, your positiveness on this subject is extraordinary. How could you drop the wallet? Do you keep it in the same pocket with your handkerchief?"

"On, no, auntie; right in here."

"And you haven't bought anything?"

"No, auntie; you wouldn't let me pay the car fare, or anything else. But still I must have taken out the wallet by mistake. You see I *know* nobody's picked my pockets."

"Why, Horace, you just said Granny picked 'em."

"No, Dot, I didn't! I only spoke of the queer way she had of leaning forward."

"But you scowled at her sharp enough to take head off."

"If I were you, Dot, I wouldn't be any more disagreeable than I was absolutely obliged to.—Now, auntie, how much does it cost to advertise?"

"A dollar or so I believe."

"Well, if you'll lend me the money, I want to do it."

"To be plain with you, Horace, I really do not think it will be of the slightest use in this case; but I will consent to it if it will be any relief to your mind.

We shall be obliged to cross the ferry again, for the advertisement ought to go into a Brooklyn paper."

"We are tired enough to drop," said Dotty; "and all these stars and things, too!"

"Yes, we are all tired; but we will leave you little girls at the ferry-house on the other side.

"But, auntie," said Prudy, anxiously, "I shouldn't really dare have the care of Fly. You know just how it is."

"Yes, I do know just how it is. Fly must walk, with her tired little feet, to the Eagle office, with Horace and me; or else she must make a solemn promise not to go out of the ferry-house."

"But I don't want to make a *solomon* promise, auntie; I want to see the eagle."

Mrs. Allen sighed. She began to think

she had undertaken a great task in inviting these children to visit her. Instead of a pleasure, they had proved, thus far, a weariness — always excepting Prudy. She, dear, self-forgetting little girl, could not fail to be a comfort wherever she went.

CHAPTER XIII.

THE PUMPKIN HOOD.

To the "Eagle" office they went — obstinate Horace, patient Aunt Madge, and between them the "blue- bottle Fly."

"I do feel right sorry, auntie," said Horace, a sudden sense of shame coming over him; "but I'm so sure I dropped the money, you know; or I wouldn't drag you up this hill when you're so tired."

A sharp answer rose to Mrs. Allen's lips, but she held it back.

"Only a boy! In a fair way to learn a useful lesson, too. Let me keep my temper! If I scold, I spoil the whole."

They entered the office, and left with the editor this advertisement :—

"Lost.—Between Prospect Park and Fulton Ferry, a porte-monnaie, marked 'Horace S. Clifford,' containing thirty-five dollars. The finder will be suitably rewarded by leaving the same at No. —, Cor. Fifth Ave. and —— Street."

"It is no matter about advertising Prudy's purse, it was so shabby," said Aunt Madge; and on their way back to the ferry-house she bought her another.

"O, thank you, auntie, darling," said Prudy; "and thank you, too, Horace, for losing my old one; it wasn't fit to be seen. And here is a whole dollar inside! O, Aunt Madge, *are* you an angel?"

"Prue, you deserve your good luck; you don't come down on a fellow, hammer and tongs, because he happens to meet with an accident."

"Horace," said Dotty, meekly, "are you willing to carry my gloves?"

"Yes, to be sure; but you don't want to go home bare-handed—do you?"

"Why, I was thinking how nice 'twould be, Horace, to have you take 'em, and lose 'em, and me have a new pair. There's a hole in the thumb."

This little sally amused everybody, and Horace had the grace not to be sensitive, though the laugh was against him.

"Another queer day," said he, when they were at last at home again. "I don't know what will become of us all, if we keep on like this."

The poor boy was trying his best to brave it out; but Aunt Madge could see that his heart was sore.

"Lost every cent I'm worth," mused he, turning his coat-pocket inside out, and scowling at it. "Got to be a beggar as long as I stay in New York!"

The whole party were tired, and Horace's gloom seemed to fill the parlor like a fog, and make even the gas look dim.

"I feel dreffly," said Fly, curling her head under her brother's arm, like a chicken under its mother's wing—a way she had when she was troubled. "I feel just zif I didn't love nobody in the world, and there didn't nobody love me."

This brought Horace around in a minute, and called forth a pickaback ride.

"Music! let us have music," said Aunt Madge, flying to the piano. "When little folks grow so cold-hearted, in my house, that they don't love anybody, it's time to warm their hearts with some happy little songs. Come, girls!"

She played a few simple tunes, and the

children all sang till the fog of gloom had disappeared, and the gas burned brightly once more.

Half an hour afterwards, just as Fly was told she ought to be sleepy, because her bye-low hymn had been sung,—" Sleep, little one, like a lamb in the fold,"—and she had answered that she " couldn't be sleepy, athout auntie would hurry quick to come in with a drink of water," there was a strange arrival. Nathaniel, the waiting man, ushered into the parlor a droll little old woman, dressed in a short calico gown, with gay figures over it as large as cabbages; calf-skin shoes; and a green pumpkin hood, with a bow on top.

" Good evening, ma'am," said Horace, rising, and offering her a chair. She did not seem to see very well, in spite of her enormous spectacles ; for she took no notice of the chair, and remained standing in the middle of the floor.

"She stares at me so hard!" thought Horace—"that's the reason she can't see anything else."—"Please take a chair, ma'am."

"Can't stop to sit down. Is your name Horace S. Clifford?" said the old woman, in a very feeble voice.

Horace looked at her; she had not a tooth in her head.

"Yes, ma'am; my name is Horace Clifford," said he, respectfully. He had great reverence for age, and could keep his mouth from twitching; but I'm sorry to say Prudy's danced up at the corners, and Dotty's opened and showed her back teeth. The woman must have had all those clothes made when she was young, for nobody

13

wore such things now; but it wasn't likely she knew that, poor soul!

"Did you go to the 'Brooklyn Eagle' office, to-day, to ad-*ver*-tise some lost money, little boy?"

"Yes, ma'am.—Why, that advertisement can't have been printed *so* quick!"

"No, I calculate not. Did you go in with a lady, and a leetle, oneasy, springy kind of a leetle girl?"

"Why, that's me," put in Fly.

"Yes, ma'am—yes; were you there? What do you know about it?"

"Don't be in a hurry, little boy. I want to be safe and sure. I expect you took notice of a young man in a bottle-green coat,—no, a greenish-black coat,—a-sittin' down by the door."

"O, I don't know. Yes, I think I did. Was he the one? Did he find the money?"

"Did you walk up Orange Street?" continued the old woman. "No, I mean Cranberry Street?"

"O, *dear*, I don't know! Prudy, run, call Aunt Madge. Please tell me, ma'am, have you got it with you? Is my name on the inside?"

"Wait till the little girl calls your aunt. Perhaps she'd be willing to let me tell the story in my own way. I'd ruther deal with grown folks," said the provoking old lady.

Horace's eyes flashed, but he contrived to keep his temper.

"It is my purse, ma'am, and my aunt knows nothing about it. I can tell you just how it looks, and all there is in it."

"Perhaps you are one of the kind that can tell folks a good deal, and thinks nobody knows things so well as yourself," returned the disagreeable old woman, smiling and showing her toothless gums. "From what I can learn, I should judge you talked ruther too loud about your money; for there was a pusson heerd you in the ferry-boat, and took pains to go in the same car afterwards, and pick your pocket."

"Pick—my—pocket?"

"Yes, your pocket. You wise, wonderful young man!"

"How? When? Where?"

"This is how," said the old woman, quick as a thought putting out her hand, and thrusting it into Horace's breast pocket.

"O, it's auntie's rings—it's auntie's rings," cried Fly, jumping up, and seizing the pretended old woman by her calico sleeve.

"Why, Aunt Madge, that isn't you!"

"But how'd you take out yer teeth?" said Fly; "your teeth? your teeth?"

"O, I didn't take them out, Miss Bright-eyes. I only put a little spruce gum over them."

"Horace, I can't find auntie anywhere in this house," said Prudy, appearing at the parlor door. "Do you suppose she's gone off and hid?"

"Yes, she's hid inside that old gown."

"What do you mean?"

"That's auntie, and her teeth's *in*," explained Fly.

"Only I wish she was an old woman, and had really brought me my money," said Horace, in a disappointed tone. "I declare, there was one time I thought the old nuisance was coming round to it, and going to give me the wallet."

"What a wise, wonderful youth!" said

the aged dame, in a cracked voice. "Thinks
I can give him his wallet, when he's got
it himself, right close to his heart."

Horace put his hand in his breast pocket.

Wonder of wonders! There was the
wallet! And not only his, but Prudy's!
Had he been asleep all day? Or was he
asleep now?

"Money safe? Not a cent gone. Hoo-
rah! Hoo-ra-ah!"

And for want of a cap to throw, he
threw up Fly.

"Where did it come from? Where did
the old woman find it? O, no; the man
in the green-bottle coat? — O, no; there
wasn't any old woman," cried the children,
hopelessly confused. "But who found the
money? Did I drop it on Cranberry
Street?" "Did he drop it on Quamby
Street?" "Who brought it?" Who
bringed it?"

THE PUMPKIN HOOD. — Page 193.

Aunt Madge stuffed her fingers into her ears. "They are all talking at once; they're enough to craze a body! They forget how old I am! Came all the way from the Eagle office, afoot and alone, with only four children to —"

"O, auntie, don't play any more! Talk sober! Talk honest! Did Horace have his pockets picked?"

"Yes, he did," replied Aunt Madge, speaking in her natural tones, and throwing off the pumpkin hood; "if you want the truth, he did."

"Why Aunt Madge Allen! It does not seem possible! Who picked my pockets?"

"Some one who heard you talking so loud about your money."

"But how could it be taken out, and I not know it?"

"Quite as easily as it could be put back, and you not know it."

"That's true, Horace Clifford! Auntie put it back, and you never knew it."

"So she did," said Horace, looking as bewildered as if he had been whirling around with his eyes shut; "so she did—didn't she? But that was because I was taken by surprise, seeing her without a tooth in her head, you know."

"You have been taken by surprise twice to-day, then," said Aunt Madge, demurely. "It is really refreshing, Horace, to find that such a sharp young man *can* be caught napping!"

"Well, I—I—I must have been thinking of something else, auntie."

"So I conclude. And you must be thinking of something else still, or you'd ask me—"

"O, yes, auntie; how did the thief happen to give it up? There, there, you

needn't say a word! I see it all in your
eyes! You took the money yourself. O,
Aunt Madge!

"Well, if that wasn't queer doings!"
cried Dotty.

"Yes, it is quite contrary to my usual
habits. I never robbed anybody before.
I hadn't the faintest idea I could do it
without Horace's knowledge."

"Why, auntie, I never was so astonished
in my life!" said the youth, looking great-
ly confused.

"I never heard of a person's being
robbed that wasn't astonished," said Aunt
Madge, with a mischievous smile. "Will
you be quite as sure of yourself another
time, think?"

"No, auntie, I shan't; that's a fact."

"That's my good, frank boy," said Aunt
Madge, kissing his forehead. "And he

won't toss his head,—just this way,—like a young lord of creation, when meddlesome aunties venture to give him advice."

Horace kissed Mrs. Allen's cheek rather thoughtfully, by way of reply.

"I don't see, Aunt Madge," said Prudy, "why you went back across the river to put that piece in the paper, when you were the one that had the money all the time."

"I did it to pacify Horace. He *knew* his pockets hadn't been picked. Besides I felt guilty. It was rather cruel in me —wasn't it?—to let him suffer so long."

"Not cruel a bit; good enough for me." cried Horace, with a generous outburst. "You're just the jolliest woman, auntie— the jolliest woman! There you are; you look so little and sweet! But if folks think they're going to get ahead of you, why, just let 'em try it, say I!"

DEAR READERS: Horace was scarcely more astonished, when his pocket was picked, than I am this minute, to find myself at the end of my book! I had very much more to tell; but now it must wait till another time.

Meanwhile the Parlins and Cliffords are "climbing the dream tree." Let us hope they are destined to meet with no more misfortunes during the rest of their stay in New York.

SOPHIE ✦ MAY'S

"LITTLE-FOLKS" BOOKS.

LEE AND SHEPARD, PUBLISHERS, BOSTON.

"The children will not be left without healthful entertainment and kindly instruction so long as SOPHIE MAY (Miss Rebecca S. Clarke) lives and wields her graceful pen in their behalf. Miss CLARKE has made a close and loving study of childhood, and she is almost idolized by the crowd of 'nephews and nieces' who claim her as aunt. Nothing to us can ever be quite so delightfully charming as were the 'Dotty Dimple' and the 'Little Prudy' books to our youthful imagination; but we have no doubt the little folks of to-day will find the story of 'Flaxie Frizzle' and her young friends just as fascinating. There is a sprightliness about all of Miss CLARKE's books that attracts the young, and their purity, their absolute cleanliness, renders them invaluable in the eyes of parents and all who are interested in the welfare of children." — *Morning Star.*

"Genius comes in with 'Little Prudy.' Compared with her, all other book-children are cold creations of literature; she alone is the real thing. All the quaintness of children, its originality, its tenderness and its teasing, its infinite uncommon drollery, the serious earnestness of its fun, the fun of its seriousness, the naturalness of its plays, and the delicious oddity of its progress, all these united for dear Little Prudy to embody them." — *North American Review,*